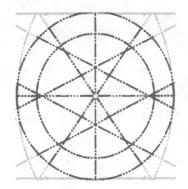

Each One a Minister

Using God's Gifts for Ministry

(Revised and Expanded)

William J. Carter

DISCIPLESHIP RESOURCES

P.O. BOX 340003 • NASHVILLE, TN 37203-0003
www.discipleshipresources.org

This revised edition of *Each One a Minister* is dedicated to

James E. Whedbee
and
Gordon Ridenour,

called and gifted associates in ministry.

Cover and book design by Nanci H. Lamar

Edited by Linda R. Whited and Heidi L. Hewitt

ISBN 0-88177-375-1

Library of Congress Catalog Card No. 2002102301

Quotations identified as *Book of Discipline* are from *The Book of Discipline of The United Methodist Church—2000.* Copyright © 2000 by The United Methodist Publishing House. Used by permission.

Scripture quotations, unless otherwise indicated, are from the *Good News Translation in Today's English Version— Second Edition.* Copyright © 1992 by American Bible Society. Used by permission.

DR375

Contents

Part I

The Church, Ministry, and Gifts

Suppose you had lived for two years in a community where you argued vehemently with members of your group, caught some of your fellow Christians practicing black magic, and started a riot over religious commercialism. If you were later writing a letter to this community, what would you say?

What you would write might depend on your maturity in the faith. While in his formative stages, Paul often became involved in controversy. His first preaching led to criticism from fellow Christians and to his banishment to Tarsus for a number of years (Acts 9:26-30). Later, he returned to ministry as a teacher with Barnabas in the Gentile church at Antioch (Acts 11:19-26) and then went on his first missionary journey with Barnabas, Silas, and John Mark (who went back home within a short while). Paul was a leader in a delegation to a conference in Jerusalem to protest the requirement that all new converts obey the ceremonial laws of Judaism (Acts 15:1-35). There a great debate between the people from Antioch and the apostles was resolved only when the apostles agreed to stop requiring new Christians to observe most of the ancient customs.

Shortly after their return to Antioch, Paul and Barnabas got into a shouting match over whether to take John Mark on the next missionary journey. The result was that each went his separate way, with Barnabas taking John Mark with him. Paul chose Silas to accompany him and later recruited Timothy from Lystra in Galatia to complete the new team (Acts 15:36–16:5).

Early in his ministry Paul wrote a letter to the Galatians in which he accuses them of deserting him and calls them "foolish Galatians" (Galatians 3:1). He hints that those who disagree with him are cursed. Later, in letters to the church at Corinth, Paul condemns those who criticize him and threatens to bring a whip and to not be lenient (1 Corinthians 4:14-21; 2 Corinthians 13:1-4). However, Paul's first letter to the Corinthians also contains the magnificent chapter on love, 1 Corinthians 13. In his letter to the Romans, he admonishes the faithful to "welcome those who are weak in faith," to "stop judging one another," and to "aim at those things that bring peace and that help strengthen one another" (Romans 14:1, 13, 19). By the time Paul wrote to the Philippians, he was even more tolerant and affectionate (Philippians 1:18-28; 3:12-21). Paul's letters from prison are gentle and persuasive. God was working mightily in him during this transition time, so we can see the work of grace as we read his words.

What you would write to your community might depend on what was happening to you at the time. Paul's letters to the Thessalonians were written while he was dealing with controversy over Christ's return. Some people were stopping their ordinary lives in order to wait for Christ, so Paul's words are directive, even sharp, in tone: "Whoever refuses to work is not allowed to eat" (2 Thessalonians 3:10). The letter to the Ephesians was written from prison. Like Paul's other prison letters, it reflects a sense of serenity and universality.

What you would write to your community might also depend on what had happened to the community since you left. The Corinthian congregation never settled down. Even at the end of the first century, another Christian letter writer, Clement, was still calling them to overcome the immaturity of pride and envy. But the church at Ephesus appears to have become a stable, stalwart group.

The letter Paul wrote to the Ephesians is sensitive, affectionate, and compassionate, reassuring the people that they are beloved of Paul and of God and that they are citizens of a wider community than they had ever imagined. Furthermore, Paul says, they are the body of Christ, just as Jesus had been the body of God; and they carry within themselves gifts of such importance that they could become the foundation for building the Body up to its intended stature.

The Foundation of the Church: The Gifts for Ministry

The early church faced a dilemma that all new organizations encounter: What was its mission, and how could it be accomplished? Paul was the spokesperson for God's design for the new fellowship.

It all began in Paul's letter to the church at Corinth. Some of the people there had asked in a letter about *pneumatikos,* a Greek word derived from *pneuma,* which is usually translated as "wind, breath, or spirit." It should be translated as "spirituality" or "spiritual matters," but it is translated as "spiritual gifts" in many versions. Paul, led by God, perceived that they were actually talking about dramatic evidences, such as speaking in tongues. Are these required for Christians to prove that they have the Holy Spirit?

Paul wrote in his letter that they do not need to worry about that. He reassures them that "no one can confess 'Jesus is Lord,' without being guided by the Holy Spirit" (1 Corinthians 12:3). So, being able to affirm that Jesus is Lord is the only proof Christians need that they have the Holy Spirit.

However, in the next paragraph, Paul says that there are manifestations of the new life in Christ that do need to be explored. He calls them *charismata,* derived from *charis,* which means grace. The meaning of charismata would be something like gifts of grace (1 Corinthians 12:7-11).

People like me who do not know Greek missed this shift for many years. Paul introduced a new Christian concept. He and God turned to a new word, not used before in Christian literature, to describe the evidence in Christian lives that they are new creatures in Christ. Paul switched the discussion from *spiritual requirements* to *signs of grace.* Instead of matters of the spirit (*pneuma*), he began to discuss matters of grace. He wrote of *pneumatikos* only six times, mostly in disapproval, but he referred to *charismata* many times. Charismata are gifts of grace by which people are prepared to do ministry. Those who have been saved by grace are prepared by grace to serve God. It is all connected.

While these gifts of grace are sometimes identified as given by the Spirit, they are also given by Jesus Christ (Ephesians 4). They come from God, the whole Trinity, as a way of preparing believers for ministry. So, throughout this book we will refer to them as *gifts for ministry.* You will learn much more about that in the study of the Book of Ephesians that follows, along with other insights into the expectations for Christians in the first century and today.

About This Book

Part 1 will guide you in studying the key New Testament concepts of *church, ministry,* and *gifts,* based on the letter to the Ephesians, with other New Testament references. Since I am convinced that the study of the New Testament is the only way to learn about Jesus Christ and the intentions of God for us, I put special emphasis on study of the text. Even though we may have read the Book of Ephesians many times, we can gain insights by studying it again that we have not seen before.

The study, divided into six sessions, is intended for either personal or group reflection. Within each session several themes are developed, each with Scripture references from the Book of Ephesians and from other sources. Be sure to read the designated chapter or verses in the Bible before reading the discussion of the topics. Then be sure to complete each of the spiritual exercises as you study. A minimum of six ninety-minute sessions is suggested (perhaps shorter for individual study, perhaps longer in some groups).

Parts 2 and 3 address the application of the gifts to ministry in our church and community. They will guide individuals or groups in recognizing and using gifts for ministry, with specific areas outlined to illustrate general principles.

Part 4 directs you to other resources you may want to explore. Some are fairly new resources.

Scripture quotations are taken from the *Good News Translation in Today's English Version—Second Edition*. You may wish to compare the texts with other translations, especially if you have favorites.

God's Intention for Us

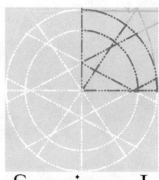

Get Ready

The Book of Ephesians is a letter rich in resources for people who desire to serve God. It is a spiritual manual designed to introduce readers to the plan of God for themselves and for the body of Christ. The six sessions in this part of the book will lead you through that resource and will help you focus on God's intentions for you and for your spiritual maturation. The lessons may be studied by someone in solitude, or they may be studied in a group of friends, in a Sunday school class, or in an organized spiritual-growth group. In any case, it would be good to start with the aim of enlarging your spiritual life. Spirituality, defined as closeness to God, is our highest goal. Christians have been on a spiritual journey much of their lives, and each day brings an opportunity to add to that voyage of faith.

Since you are starting a spiritual-growth adventure, it would be good to review your past spiritual life, tracing how you came to be where you are now. The spiritual exercise below will help you review and will give you a starting point for this study.

A Spiritual Exercise: The P-Square

Draw a four-part square on a sheet of paper. Label each part as one item in your spiritual journey: person, place, period, passion.

Then fill in each square with the important experiences of your own spiritual life.

1. A person important in your spiritual journey (parent, pastor, friend)

2. A place where spiritual growth occurred (home, church, school, camp)

3. A period when spiritual change was evident (a date, a year, or a stage in life such as youth, young adult, school years, yesterday, today)

4. A passion that was important at some point in your journey (a cause, an idea, an action)

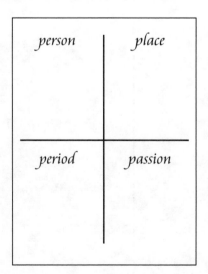

If you are alone, spend some time reflecting on the significance of the spiritual experiences you have listed—and on others that may come to mind.

If you are in a group, divide into groups of three or four. Let each person explain the meaning of one of the squares of his or her P-Square. (Take no more than 90 seconds for each person.) Then let anyone who wishes tell about other squares until the time is up (about 10 minutes).

At the conclusion, ask if anyone would like to tell, in a sentence or two, what he or she heard another person say. (No one can tell his or her own story.) Notice the varieties of spiritual experiences remembered.

End the discussion with these questions:

• Is it good for people to talk with others about their spiritual experiences?

• What values are there in this spiritual exercise?

God's Intention

All of Paul's letters include an affectionate greeting. Even to the church at Corinth, which was a troublesome congregation, Paul begins with a loving statement: "I always give thanks to my God for you" (1 Corinthians 1:4).

> *Ever since I heard of your faith in the Lord Jesus and your love for all of God's people, I have not stopped giving thanks to God for you.*
>
> (EPHESIANS 1:15-16)

The Ephesians, too, are made to feel loved and appreciated by his comment on their faith in the opening paragraphs of the letter to them.

In our relationships with other Christians, we can practice this personal affirmation. Paul demonstrates that we can express affection and positive appreciation even for those with whom we have disagreements.

Carl Rogers, a teacher of counseling, used the phrase *unconditional positive regard*—a respect not dependent on behavior—to describe what one person can offer another in times of stress. Unconditional positive regard has occasionally been a problem that I have tried to work on. A number of times I have been asked to write letters to someone entering an Emmaus Walk (a spiritual renewal program of The Upper Room). It was a good exercise for me in practicing unconditional affirmation. The following is a good spiritual exercise for you.

A Spiritual Exercise: A Letter to My Church

If you were writing a letter to the members of your congregation, what affirming words would you say to them? Write a few sentences or phrases you might use.

_____

_____

_____

_____

_____

_____

_____

_____

_____

_____

If you are studying in a group, you might want to talk together about some of these thoughts.

The early Christians tried to understand how Jesus Christ fit into the history of the world and the plan of God. Of course, most of the earliest Christians were Jews. Faithful Jews had worshiped one God for many generations and had developed ceremonial practices, which they revered. For them, the new faith was a continuation of the old. Jesus was the Messiah expected by the prophets, but he did not exactly fit the old image. His kingdom was spiritual rather than political; the freedom he brought was from religious legalism rather than from the laws of the state; and his power was directed against evil in the hearts of people rather than against the enemies of Israel. Still, the Jewish Christians believed that he was the Messiah and Savior.

Now the Gentiles were learning about the one God and Jesus Christ at the same time. The Gentile Christians had difficulty seeing their place in the new faith. Peter and Paul and a host of others had been preaching to them, but not everyone agreed. Many had accepted Christ as their personal Savior, but some people wondered where they belonged in the whole people of God. How could they possibly be included in the inner circle?

The Christians, both Jew and Gentile, wondered what difference the coming of Jesus had made.

- Was the worship of God, or the manner of serving God, now to be changed?
- How did Jesus connect to the experience of the Jewish people and to the faith explained in the religious writing of the Hebrew Scriptures (which Christians now call the Old Testament)?
- What were Christians supposed to do?
- Burnt offerings were no longer important. What was important?

A Spiritual Exercise: Foundations of Faith

List some important factors in the history of Israel: events, people, and experiences from the Old Testament. Take about five minutes.

_____

_____

_____

_____

When you have finished, put the items in approximate chronological order. (Many Bible commentaries will have a timeline to help you.)

_____

_____

_____

_____

If you are doing this exercise in a group, combine the individual lists by having someone write them on a chalkboard or on newsprint.

Choose the five most important items.

1. _____

2. _____

3. _____

4. _____

5. _____

- Are these five among the foundations of the faith of the Old Testament?
- Are they mentioned or implied in the New Testament?

Take ten to fifteen minutes for this discussion.

In Ephesians 1:8-10, Paul explains that a secret has been revealed: There really is no problem. Jesus came not only to the people of Israel but also to all people—everyone who would accept him as the presence of God in the world. In fact, Paul says, it is God's intention that all creation be brought together.

In all his wisdom and insight God did what he had purposed, and made known to us the secret plan he had already decided to complete by means of Christ. This plan, which God will complete when the time is right, is to bring all creation together, everything in heaven and on earth, with Christ as head.

(EPHESIANS 1:8-10)

Everything is to be under the lordship of Christ, even though we humans often seem to be working to separate rather than to unite. The aim of God's plan is to reconcile all of these elements. God is making a new Jerusalem, a global spiritual city. Nothing is to be left out. God is drawing the whole world into one circle, and no one can permanently interfere. As Paul puts it in his letter to the church at Rome, "Nothing can separate us from his love: neither death nor life, neither angels nor other heavenly rulers or powers, neither the present nor the future, neither the world above nor the world below—there is nothing in all creation that will ever be able to separate us from the love of God which is ours through Christ Jesus our Lord" (Romans 8:38-39).

Each of us also has a story that includes our relationship to God. What are our own foundations?

A Spiritual Exercise: Remembering My Life Story

Choose four to six titles of chapters in an imaginary book entitled *Chapters in My Life Story*. Be sure to include times of spiritual growth or change. For instance, I might write the chapter title "A Slanted Beginning," because I was born in Slant, Virginia, and learned about Jesus in the Slant Methodist Sunday school. What are your chapter titles?

1. _____
2. _____
3. _____
4. _____
5. _____
6. _____

Reflect on these titles. If you are doing this study in a group, get with three or four other people to talk about the chapters in your book. Allow two minutes per person. After all have had a chance to tell their chapter titles, allow time for questions and brief explanations of individual titles.

• Do these titles include foundation stones of your faith development?
• If you are in a group, consider the experiences others have mentioned. Do you and others in the group have some of the same or similar foundation stones?

The Hebrews had a special relationship with God. They called themselves the chosen people because they were convinced that they had been selected for a purpose greater than their importance as a nation. Through good and bad times, their best leaders always called them back to that vision. The image of a chosen people was a symbol of their identify as a people. They held onto it, even when they did not think that they were living up to its highest ideals.

Now there was a new factor: Jesus Christ had died on the cross. Those who believed that he was God's redeemer and followed his way were counted as God's people. They were not necessarily the same ethnic group as those who called themselves the chosen. How could these new believers know that they were God's people too?

Paul answered the question in a simple way: The Spirit is the guarantee (Ephesians 1:13-14). To the church at Rome, Paul wrote these words on the same subject: "God's Spirit joins himself to our spirits to declare that we are God's children" (Romans 8:16).

The choice is up to us individually; but, as we choose God, God also chooses us. "You believed in Christ," Paul says, "and God put his stamp of ownership on you by giving you the Holy Spirit he had promised" (Ephesians 1:13). The believer is chosen for a special relationship and made a part of God's household.

A Spiritual Experience: Being Chosen

Reflect on a special time when you were chosen by a playground team, by a job supervisor, by someone in marriage, and so forth.

1. How did you know you had been chosen?

2. How did it make you feel?

Now examine your relationship to God.
1. Do you think you have been chosen by God?

2. How do you feel about that now?

If you are in a group, talk about your answers
with another person or in a small group.

Paul explains in great detail just how marvelous it is to be God's adopted children. He says he hopes we will know "how rich are the wonderful blessings he promises his people" (Ephesians 1:18). Finally, he reminds the Ephesians (and us) that the church is the result of the work of Christ and that the church (the people of God) is expected to complete that work: "God put all things under Christ's feet and gave him to the church as supreme Lord over all things. The church is Christ's body, the completion of him who himself completes all things everywhere" (Ephesians 1:22-23).

What does it mean for us to be the body of Christ? It is this theme we will pursue to the end of this study. It is clear that Paul's letter to the Ephesians was intended to help the early Christians become the body of Christ. It was designed to give guidance in Christian ministry, helping us understand what things we may be able to do and the spirit in which we are to do them.

PREPARED FOR GOOD DEEDS

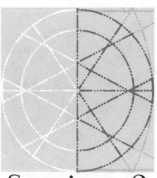

"**I**t is by God's grace that you have been saved" (Ephesians 2:5). So begins Paul's explanation of the purpose and progress of the Christian life. While the overall plan of God is to bring everything together with Christ as its head, it is necessary to remember that the first step in that process is justification, getting right with God.

We are born in sin, and our every effort to escape sin fails until the grace of God enters our life. And that grace is available only through God's action. We cannot earn it, force it, or take credit for it. "For it is by God's grace that you have been saved through faith. It is not the result of your own efforts, but God's gift, so that no one can boast about it" (Ephesians 2:8).

However, it is through faith that this miracle of grace is made possible. Some would have us believe that God's grace is totally unrelated to our personal choices, and that we are predestined from birth for either salvation or damnation at God's whim, with no initiative from us. This belief, though, makes any effort toward evangelism useless. If there is nothing a person can do that affects his or her justification, then we cannot help that person.

> *It is by God's grace that you have been saved through faith. It is not the result of your own efforts, but God's gift, so that no one can boast about it. God has made us what we are, and in our union with Christ Jesus he has created us for a life of good deeds, which he has already prepared for us to do.*
>
> (EPHESIANS 2:8-10)

SPIRITUAL EXERCISE: CLAIMING GRACE THROUGH CHRIST

Write a brief account of a time (or times) when you realized that God's grace had entered your life.

_____

_____

_____

_____

How do you feel about your relationship with God right now?

_____

_____

_____

_____

If you are in a group, talk aloud about what you have written.
(Be considerate, as some may be uncomfortable talking about these things.)

This Bible passage, however, implies that one human action does affect the process: *faith*. When we have faith in Jesus Christ, we become open to God's grace. In another letter, Paul is even more explicit: "It is through faith that all of you are God's children in union with Christ Jesus.... For when we are in union with Christ Jesus, neither circumcision nor the lack of it makes any difference at all; what matters is faith that works through love" (Galatians 3:26; 5:6).

While we can take no credit for having faith, it is necessary for us to take the step of faith to experience that marvelous grace (*charis*) that is God's free gift to those who open themselves to it. This theme predominates throughout the letters of Paul. Without God's use of Paul as the interpreter of the meaning of justification and salvation, we would still be unclear about it; and perhaps the faith would have expired in its infancy.

Works do matter. For a good part of Christian history, the value of works (good deeds) has been in dispute. People have often disdained works theology. Since works will not save us, many have concluded that good deeds are worthless in the Christian life and that only faith counts.

However, there is more to the story. In Ephesians 2:10, immediately after stressing that works are useless in obtaining salvation, Paul tells us that "God has made us what we are, and in our union with Christ Jesus *he has created us for a life of good deeds [works]*, which he has already prepared for us to do" (emphasis added). Surely that is meant to connect our theology with our practice. We are not only expected to do good deeds but were actually created to accomplish them. The presence of Christ in our lives motivates us toward good works. It gives us both the urge and the means to do them. The absence of good works may be a sign that our faith is not yet fulfilled.

Some have argued that God always intended that God's people perform acts of love and mercy. As proof they point to the comments of Jesus about loving neighbors as ourselves (Luke 10:27); to the story of the Last Judgment (Matthew 25:31-46), with its stress on food, a drink of water, a visit to prison or the sick bed; and to Paul's comments on owing no one anything but love, for "to love...is to obey the whole Law" (Romans 13:8-10). John Wesley's General Rules include not only works of piety that maintain one's relationship with God but also works of mercy that show one's love and care for neighbors.

While there have been times when the church has not given attention to the needs of the world around it, a renewed spirit of servanthood seems to be emerging now. During the past few years, denominations that have historically claimed evangelism as their only task, while carefully avoiding being identified with social action, have proclaimed—even in TV ads—their involvement in community service and justice. We may also observe that some who have been content with good works are learning to offer Christ in ways that touch the errant heart. We are discovering that John Wesley's union of justification by faith and going on to perfection does describe the biblical understanding of the life of those in Christ. We are both believers and doers, people of both faith and good works. Either is barren by itself, as the letter of James reminds us: "Faith without actions is dead" (James 2:26).

But what about the phrase "which he has already prepared for us to do"? Does it mean that God has set the course of our lives so that we will do only what he has required? Has he set up a program that we must follow automatically?

I think not. Instead, I believe these words imply that as we become God's redeemed, God places or strengthens special abilities and inclinations within us that can be drawn forth when needed to do the ministry expected of God's people. When the time is right, God calls us to be in ministry using these inner qualities, the _gifts for ministry_, that prepare us for service. All Christians are gifted. All may be called at appropriate times to use their gifts. This process will be examined further in Ephesians 4, where Paul gives a comprehensive statement of the meaning and purpose of the gifts of ministry.

> *So then, you Gentiles are not foreigners or strangers any longer; you are now citizens together with God's people and members of the family of God.*
>
> (EPHESIANS 2:19)

It is no accident that the next subject of Paul's letter is the oneness of all Christians. From the beginning, divisiveness has been a problem. Since we are so divided, as were the earliest Christians, we must seek the source of our unity. What makes us one body?

The first answer is that through the work of Christ, all barriers have been broken down. "For Christ himself has brought us peace by making Jews and Gentiles one people. With his own body he broke the wall that separated them and kept them enemies.... By means of the cross he united both races into one body" (Ephesians 2:14, 16).

Christians have sometimes missed the importance of that idea. For the people of Jesus' day, there were only two kinds of people in the world, Jews and Gentiles. For them "both races" meant *all* races, since Gentiles comprise everyone who is not Jewish. The death of Jesus Christ has destroyed *all* distinctions of race and nationality. Wherever people are and whatever their background, they are now one people. It would have been good if we had understood that earlier in Christian history. It would be good if we really understood it now.

The second answer is that we are united even though we do different things for Christ. The differences do not matter. As individuals, groups, and denominations, we are gifted in various ways; yet we can all belong to the Body as long as we are serving the head, Jesus Christ. Individuals and denominations need not fight over their differences. They can rejoice that God has called each to do separate ministries, which, when combined, express the work of God.

Of course, there are Christians and non-Christians, but for the first time everyone has *access* to God. "It is through Christ that all of us, Jews and Gentiles, are able to come in the one Spirit into the presence of the Father" (Ephesians 2:18). No one is outside the grace of God. There is no preparation necessary, no clubs to join, no rituals to go through. Every human being is a brother or sister and potentially a fellow believer. That makes all of us of the same worth.

We are fellow citizens, Paul reminds us. Even if we are of different races or speak different languages, we are the same in Christ, citizens of the same spiritual realm. "In union with him you too are being built together with all the others into a place where God lives through his Spirit" (Ephesians 2:22).

Sharing the Secret

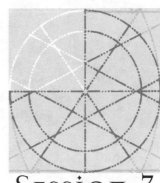

The secret is out—Jesus Christ has become the source of a new personal salvation and the center of a new universal kinship. We are all one body, one spirit, one race. Nothing can separate us from the love of God.

Such news must be made public. Paul explains that he was made a servant of the gospel in order to take the message of the infinite riches of Christ to all people. Being in prison is not too steep a price to pay for the opportunity of telling others this secret. In fact, it may turn out to be an advantage. In his letter to the church at Philippi, Paul says that the things that have happened to him "have really helped the progress of the gospel" (Philippians 1:12).

Making the story known is the responsibility of each disciple, regardless of personal circumstances. It is also a responsibility of the whole Body, the church. Paul tells the Ephesians that it is "by means of the gospel" that the secret of universal spiritual kinship has been revealed (Ephesians 3:6). He goes on to say that "by means of the church" this newfound truth will be made known everywhere (Ephesians 3:10). Even the heavenly powers will learn it through the church. (Imagine that!) Just as Jesus told the disciples

> *God, who is the Creator of all things, kept his secret hidden through all the past ages, in order that at the present time, by means of the church, the angelic rulers and powers in the heavenly world might learn of his wisdom in all its different forms.*
>
> (Ephesians 3:9-10)

A Spiritual Exercise: Friends

Compare These Statements

God has made us what we are, and in our union with Christ Jesus he has created us for a life of good deeds, which he has already prepared for us to do.

(Ephesians 2:10)

All this is done by God, who through Christ changed us from enemies into his friends [reconciled us] and gave us the task of making others his friends also.

(2 Corinthians 5:18)

Answer These Questions

1. How are making friends and doing good deeds alike?

2. How are they different?

3. What does this say about the ministry of the people of God?

to go into the world and make disciples, Paul now adds that making disciples is more than preaching, and the whole church is responsible for making God's secret known in a multitude of ways.

Sometimes we all seem to be waiting to see whose turn it is to do acts of ministry. We divide ourselves up into competing groups, each with its own agenda. Our chief motivation seems to be turning others into clones of ourselves or rejecting them as unworthy. Even within our denominations we want to do our own thing, maintaining our traditions and keeping to the same program. We sometimes even accuse one another of being traitors if we try something new in our churches. In my own denomination, I have heard people say, "But that's not really Methodist," if someone wants to try a new ministry concept or sing different songs.

According to Paul, it is always our turn. We are always up to bat. Ministry is for the here and now. It varies from place to place and from time to time, but it is always proper for Christians to be in ministry of all kinds, whether of proclaiming the word or demonstrating its application to the needs of the community. When we have become reconciled (made friends) with God, we are always expected to be making friends for Jesus (doing the ministry of reconciliation) or serving through acts of ministry.

Paul concludes this thought by reminding us of the variety of ministries: "I pray that you may have your roots and foundation in love, so that you, together with all God's people, may have the power to understand how broad and long, how high and deep, is Christ's love" (Ephesians 3:17-18).

The final prayer sums up the whole concept: "To him who by means of his power working in us is able to do so much more than we can ever ask for, or even think of: to God be the glory in the church and in Christ Jesus…forever and ever!" (Ephesians 3:20-21).

A Spiritual Exercise: Church and Community Ministries

Make a list of local church and community activities you have observed, heard about, or read about that could be called ministries. If you are meeting with a group, write the headings (see right column) on a chalkboard or newsprint and list each ministry under the appropriate heading.

Headings
1. Church activities directed to church members
2. Church activities directed to the community
3. Personal activities or projects by church people
4. Activities originating outside the church

If you are working alone, label each item with the number of the appropriate category.

Now ask yourself (or your group) the following:
1. Which of these activities are effective in expressing ministry?
2. What percentage of activities is directed outward from the church?
3. In which of these am I a participant?
4. What other ministries would help us express God's love?

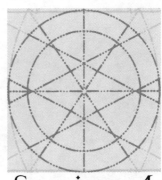

GIFTED CHILDREN

In one little gem of spiritual expression (Ephesians 4:4-6), Paul summarizes the nature of the Christian community. It is one. Anything else is incomplete. Throughout the Letter to the Ephesians, Paul refers to the church as the body of Christ. He never really explains what he means, assuming that his readers already know. Could the reason for their familiarity with the idea be that they have already heard about it or read about it in an earlier letter? Possibly so. The Letter to the Ephesians is among those written near the end of Paul's ministry, when he was in prison. First Corinthians, in which Paul explains the body of Christ in more detail, was written a number of years earlier, and the letter to Rome was sent before Paul's last trip there and his imprisonment. We know that many of the letters were circulated among the churches long before they became part of the New Testament. It seems that the concept of the church as a body probably was so widely accepted that it no longer needed to be explained. Is that still true with us?

For some of us, the image of the church as a body has lost its clarity. A rereading of Chapters 12 through 14 in 1 Corinthians can help us recapture some of its meaning. There we learn a number of things about bodies that are also true about the church. Take some time now to complete the spiritual exercise on this page.

> *There is one body and one Spirit, just as there is one hope to which God has called you. There is one Lord, one faith, one baptism; there is one God and Father of all people, who is Lord of all, works through all, and is in all.*
>
> (EPHESIANS 4:4-6)

A SPIRITUAL EXERCISE: DEFINING THE BODY

- Read 1 Corinthians 12:12-30.
- List five ways that Paul says the church is like a body. (The first comparison is done for you.)
1. It has many parts but is still a single unit.

2. _____

3. _____

4. _____

5. _____

- Can you name ways that Paul did not mention?

_____

_____

_____

- Compare your list with the lists of others.

_____

_____

If the church is like a body, it ought to have hands and feet and a heart and a language. Even as hands and feet and a heart are the means by which the body moves itself in its environment, so language is the means by which it communicates with others. *The language of the body of Christ is ministry.* Ministry tells others who the Body is and what it does. More than words, more than an affirmation of faith, the church expresses itself through ministry with and to people. Ministry is the church's way of revealing the secret. Indeed, we are all ministers, each gifted with special qualities with which we help complete the Body.

> *Each one of us has received a special gift in proportion to what Christ has given.*
>
> (EPHESIANS 4:7)

The people at Ephesus might well have said, "So we are to be in ministry. Just how do we do that?" How has God prepared us for good deeds? Or they might have said, "Some people are so good at doing things in the church that the rest of us feel inadequate. Why not let them do it?" A few might have said, "What really matters is whether you can prove your faith by showing the signs of the Holy Spirit: Two or three of our members seem to be able to heal, one or two can work miracles, and a few can speak in unknown tongues. Wouldn't it be better if we all tried to learn to do those things instead of fooling around with this other stuff?"

Paul had already dealt with issues like these at Corinth. Although Paul himself spoke in tongues, he had been especially hard on the people who put an inappropriately high value on speaking in strange tongues: "In church worship I would rather speak five words that can be understood, in order to teach others, than speak thousands of words in strange tongues" (1 Corinthians 14:19).

He also pointed out that everyone cannot expect the same gifts: "They are not all apostles or prophets or teachers. Not everyone has the power to work miracles or to heal diseases or to speak in strange tongues or to explain what is said. Set your hearts, then, on the more important gifts" (1 Corinthians 12:29-31). Note that he counts the exotic gifts as among the least important.

A Spiritual Exercise: Love

Write a sentence or two about an experience that made you feel that another person loved you. (2 minutes)

_____

_____

_____

_____

What made you feel loved? Be specific. (1 minute)

_____

_____

_____

Do you recall ever knowing that you had made someone else feel loved? If so, write a phrase or two that will help you recall it. (2 minutes)

_____

_____

_____

If you are in a group, take seven or eight minutes to talk with one another about your insights. (Each person should be limited to a minute or so.)

The best gift of all is love (1 Corinthians 13:13). In the Letter to the Ephesians, Paul mentions love again: "Be always humble, gentle, and patient. Show your love by being tolerant with one another" (Ephesians 4:2). Unity is important and is impossible without love and tolerance.

It may be that Paul intended for us to understand that love is the only gift that needs to be possessed by everyone. Certainly he prized it above everything else. And it is a gift. Not everyone knows how to express love, and hardly anyone can show it all the time.

Many barriers have always existed to the full expression of love: selfishness, a lack of appreciation of others, personality traits, external circumstances, competitiveness, prejudice, greed, and so forth. But Paul emphasizes the positive. It can be done. People can express love. It has been done. Already our lives are filled with love, if we can only bring the evidence to mind.

In at least three letters, Paul declares that we each have a gift (or gifts) that makes us special. Because we are all children of God, we are all gifted. Paul declares in Ephesians 4:7 that we are provided gifts by Christ, while in other places the gifts seem to be from the Holy Spirit. Obviously, they are from God. The effort to assign gift giving only to that part of the Trinity called the Holy Spirit may be misleading. It implies that gifts come from a particular aspect of God. Paul seems to be saying that the source of the gifts is the fullness of God—in creation, redemption, and continuing presence—and the objective is that these gifts be shared by all.

We are gifted people. Each of us has been provided something valuable for a special purpose. How to recognize our own giftedness and use it for the purpose God intended is the focus of discipleship. The names of the gifts do not seem to have been a major concern to Paul. In four passages Paul refers to specific gifts, but the lists are not the same. Sometimes it is a little difficult to determine what is meant by a particular word. Paul gives almost no definition of any of them. However, this may not be a problem; it may actually help us. It implies that the gifts are unlimited. No one has named them all, and perhaps no one should. Each of us may have the potential for a unique gift simply because each is unique.

A study of the biblical list is helpful in understanding what a gift is and how it may be applied. Turn to page 24 to read more about the lists in the Bible.

A Spiritual Exercise: A New Way of Looking at the Gifts

In the list below, check 2 to 4 items that you think you are good at. (If you do not check any, you are too modest. But don't check too many. Identify those things that you are especially good at.)

I am especially good at

- ☐ 1. Explaining things to people
- ☐ 2. Telling others about the faith
- ☐ 3. Tending to other people's needs
- ☐ 4. Helping people understand one another
- ☐ 5. Communicating in dramatic ways
- ☐ 6. Taking charge when needed
- ☐ 7. Understanding the meaning of things
- ☐ 8. Making people feel cared for
- ☐ 9. Giving graciously
- ☐ 10. Speaking before groups
- ☐ 11. Making unusual things happen
- ☐ 12. Identifying religious frauds
- ☐ 13. Encouraging and supporting others
- ☐ 14. Gathering and using information
- ☐ 15. Listening and/or acting sympathetically
- ☐ 16. Helping people become healthy
- ☐ 17. Maintaining calm in times of stress
- ☐ 18. Arranging meetings and programs
- ☐ 19. Leading beyond the local church

If you are in a group, first ask for one item someone has checked. Find out how many others checked that item. Repeat a few times to see how you are alike or different in the gifts you possess.

The Ephesians were probably already acquainted with the concept of gifts, just as they were with the image of the church as the body of Christ. Paul reminds them of the variety of these gifts and then passes swiftly on to explain their purpose. He implies here and in other passages (Romans 12; 1 Corinthians 12) that *it is the very variety of the gifts that makes the body powerful.* Unity does not mean conformity; it means solidarity within diversity. We all do different things within a single mission. Oneness is of the overall purpose, not the details.

A Spiritual Exercise: Looking Closer at Biblical Gifts

Read these portions of letters from Paul to find the gifts listed there:

Romans 12:6-8   1 Corinthians 12:4-11, 27-31   Ephesians 4:11-12

Using the list below, identify the corresponding gift from the New Testament for each of the gifts you identified for yourself on page 23. (The numbers match.)

1. Teaching
2. Witness/evangelism
3. Serving/helping
4. Interpretation
5. Speaking in tongues
6. Leadership
7. Wisdom/understanding

8. Pastoring (shepherding)
9. Giving
10. Preaching/prophecy
11. Miracles
12. Discerning true and false spirits
13. Encouragement (exhortation)

14. Knowledge
15. Kindness (compassion)
16. Healing
17. Faith
18. Administration
19. Apostleship

Do you agree with the definition given for each of the gifts you have identified?

Do people in the group think they or others have any of these gifts?
When gifts are mentioned that are not included on the list, add them. (10 minutes)
Conclude by writing in one sentence your own definition of each of the gifts. Or if you are with others, divide into groups of three or four and allocate the list equally among the groups. Then talk about your answers.

He did this to prepare all God's people for the work of Christian service, in order to build up the body of Christ.

(EPHESIANS 4:12)

People are provided gifts for the good of the Body. Gifts are used properly only when they build up the fellowship, the service, the worship, the stewardship of the whole congregation and community. Although each person is gifted, the purpose is that all be enabled to minister.

From this base we can begin to glimpse a new definition of the body of Christ. It is actually the sum of its members' gifts. God has placed the gifts within the members of the church because God has ministries that the Body needs to accomplish. Each church is unique. None has the exact same purpose as any others. To discover the mission of any church, we must discover the gifts of its members. *Ministry must be based on the gifts, rather than the gifts forced to fit the ministry defined by a council or denomination.* We are not just volunteers in the program of the church; we are ministers who are answering the call of God. Out of the response to these calls comes the mission of the church. Organization must follow mission.

The Book of Discipline of The United Methodist Church—2000 defines church organization this way: "The local church shall be organized so that it can pursue its primary task and mission in the context of its own community" (¶ 242). What the church does should not be determined by a general church program or by outside organizations of any kind. Both mission and structure should come from the gifts and the calls within the Body in its own community. The New Testament speaks of making disciples as the primary task of the Body. Some have interpreted this as evangelism, but discipleship is infinitely greater than evangelism. Discipleship includes the whole range of avenues of preparing people to serve God. It is to this task that each person and the structures of the local church are called.

> *When each separate part works as it should, the whole body grows and builds itself up through love.*
>
> (EPHESIANS 4:16)

The Ephesians are reminded that we *all* have gifts, for all kinds of gifts are necessary to make the Body whole. Every person is gifted—not merely the professional church workers—and all are called to use their gifts in ministry.

We sometimes use the phrase "called to preach" when we mean "called to minister." Not all clergy are called to preach. Some are called to teach, some to pastor, some to administer, some to serve, and some to evangelize. While professional church leaders may do many official things, they also have specific gifts and specific calls to use their gifts. Claiming gifts is the beginning of true ministry for professional ministers, just as it is with the laity.

Discovering our gifts may be a lifelong process. For some of us, identifying the gifts may come easily; for others, it may be a difficult and extended task. Paul recognized that we are children in the faith and that growing up may take a long time. But eventually, if we keep trying, and if we ask our brothers and sisters in the faith to help us, we can recognize our gifts and claim them.

Of course, there is also the call of God. However gifted we are, we may not be exercising our gift at any particular time, or even know what gift we possess. That is not a handicap. The gifts are activated as God calls us to be in ministry. So, *the gifts must be coupled with the call to become effective in the Body.*

We would do well to remember that any person, clergy or lay, may be called at any time to a gift or a ministry. All have gifts to share. As I said earlier, the gifts are not limited by the lists taken from the Scriptures.

A SPIRITUAL EXERCISE: FINDING MISSION FROM GIFTS DISCOVERY

Make a list of gifts that you believe people or groups in your church may have. Are these gifts for ministry?

_____

_____

_____

_____

Develop a statement of purpose, or mission, for your church using the list you have made.

_____

_____

_____

_____

What can we discern from the presence of ministry gifts among us?

_____

_____

These lists are only illustrative, not exhaustive. The value of each gift is the same, because all are necessary to make a whole Body. Each one is priceless. Only when we recognize and affirm the value of each gift will the Body truly fit together.

Keeping the gifts of ministry in the minds of the people of the Body is one of the primary tasks of church leaders. If they do not perform that task, then every Christian must personally take up the challenge of seeking gifts and hearing calls. We are a body, not a collection of disparate parts; and what one fails to do, another should do. It is everyone's task to do the work of ministry and to give others an opportunity to share in the process from beginning to end.

> *Since you are God's dear children, you must try to be like him. Your life must be controlled by love, just as Christ loved us and gave his life for us as a sweet-smelling offering and sacrifice that pleases God.*
>
> (EPHESIANS 5:1)

While Ephesians 5:1 is out of sequence with today's text, it is completely in keeping with Paul's understanding of the context of the gifts. In 1 Corinthians 13, he calls love the greatest gift of all and gives a whole chapter over to defining it and its place in the Christian life. In Romans, he ends his discussion of the gifts by saying, "Love must be completely sincere. Hate what is evil, hold on to what is good. Love one another warmly as Christians, and be eager to show respect for one another" (Romans 12:9-10). I think he meant to say that without the atmosphere of love, the gifts are merely human qualities without any relationship to the building up of the church. It is love that gives them relevance and power. Love is the best way, and may be the only way, in which the potential of the gifts can be fully realized within the Body. We cannot stress too strongly that there is no place for grudging service or impersonal performance. The gifts are always practiced in love and always express the love that God brought to us in Christ.

THE RIGHT STUFF

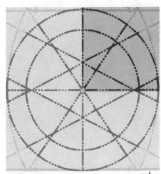

In Ephesians 4 and 5, we encounter one of the problems of the division of the Scriptures into verses and chapters. For hundreds of years, the Bible texts did not include these divisions. Chapters first appeared in the early 1200's, but it was not until the 1550's that the chapters were divided into verses. The Geneva Bible, an English translation in 1560, was the first complete printed Bible using the divisions that continue to this day. The translators often separated the text without reference to subject matter, so topics are changed in the middle of a chapter, and sometimes in the middle of a sentence. For clarity, we have reunited the subjects for our next two study sessions as follows: Ephesians 4:17–5:20, "The Right Stuff," will be Session 5. "Submit to One Another," Session 6, will start at 5:21. That should help us understand the subjects of the text.

The right stuff includes moral and ethical living. It involves us in proper relationships among ourselves and with God. The discovery of our gifts and the practice of ministry always take place in the context of a commitment to the highest ideals of Christian living. Ministry by itself is not sufficient. The service of God has a deep, personal, moral dimension that cannot be ignored, even when the work itself seems to produce good results. That means that spectacular effects do not always denote the special approval of God on a project or on its originator. Some good works precede from corrupt hearts.

That truth is one of the conditions of Christian service that modern servants sometimes seem to forget or ignore. Whether it is in the area of personal moral behavior, acceptance of people of other races or cultures, the use of language, anger, truthfulness, or indecent thoughts, we are responsible for keeping our lives free of the appearance of evil. A generation ago, some of the most popular preachers on radio used their pulpits for anti-Semitism and racial intolerance. Today many of the hate groups in the United States hide under the umbrella of the Bible and Christian rhetoric. No matter how many zealous followers they attract, they are still enemies of the faith and perverters of the true gospel.

Paul even warns us, "Do not use harmful words, but only helpful words, the kind that build up and provide what is needed, so that what you say will do good to those who hear you" (Ephesians 4:29). When I recall what I have heard some church people say about one another, or about some church activity they did not like, I wonder that we ever survived as a body. Valid criticism may be helpful, but negativism can be immoral and destructive. The least we can do is support the work of ministry by giving positive support for the best efforts of members of the Body to serve the Lord.

But the hardest constraint may be to "get rid of all bitterness, passion, and anger. No more shouting or insults, no more hateful feelings of any sort. Instead, be kind and tenderhearted to one another, and forgive one another, as God has

> *Your hearts and minds must be made completely new, and you must put on the new self, which is created in God's likeness and reveals itself in the true life that is upright and holy.*
>
> (EPHESIANS 4:23-24)

forgiven you through Christ" (Ephesians 4:31-32). The clear implication of these words is that the earliest Christians had to be warned not to do these things, so they must have been guilty of them. I am constantly reminded of that when I listen to certain religious television programs. It seems that every other sentence condemns someone with a different opinion, and that the sole message being proclaimed is that the speaker is right and everyone else is wrong and should be punished. Come to think of it, I hear some things like that in other places too. Some Christians consider tenderheartedness to be a weakness. They do not have any compassion for those who are different, and they loudly insist that all contrary opinions and practices must be stamped out, and the sooner the better.

The stuff of which the Christian life is made is "a rich harvest of every kind of goodness, righteousness, and truth" (Ephesians 5:9). Pleasing the Lord should be the chief aim of every disciple. The search for God's will for our lives never ends. The fulfillment of our ministry always lies before us. We are constantly going on toward perfection.

In the business world, we sometimes admire a certain ruthlessness and overlook tactics that wound others. We reason that they fall within the bounds of legality—barely—and are acceptable as long as they produce profits. In the world of the spirit, though, there is no such permissiveness. Paul says, "Your life must be controlled by love" (Ephesians 5:2). "You may be sure that no one who is immoral, indecent, or greedy (for greed is a form of idolatry) will ever receive a share in the Kingdom of Christ and of God" (Ephesians 5:5).

A Spiritual Exercise: Our Highest Values

Make a list of some important values that you think are essential in living the Christian life. They may be drawn from Scripture, experience, or personal convictions. If you are in a group, make a combined list.

_____

_____

_____

Choose the five most important of these values and write them down.

1. _____
2. _____
3. _____
4. _____
5. _____

If you are in a group, compare your list with the lists of others.
• How many values are the same?

_____

• What are the top five when all these are added together?

1. _____
2. _____
3. _____
4. _____
5. _____

The Christian life has many important values, but Paul has pointed out to us that some are more important than others. Love, for instance, is the highest relational value; prophecy (witnessing) is the highest communication value; forgiveness is the highest unity value. We too may find that we have to put our values in priority order. Church and people sometimes break apart over the most transitory and peripheral issues: fashions of worship, the meanings of obscure words, methods of baptism, opinions about the pastor, what women should wear to worship, who will direct the Christmas pageant. At the same time, the weightier issues of ministry and mission hardly receive attention from anyone. When we focus on ministry, though, other matters become less important and less divisive.

"Don't be fools, then, but try to find out what the Lord wants you to do" (Ephesians 5:17). The meaning is clear: First of all, don't worry about anyone else. Concentrate on God's will for your life. Let God's way be your way. Lend yourself to the ministry to which *you* are called, using the gifts with which *you* have been endowed. Everyone can have plenty to do, whatever their deficiencies or gifts. Nobody is perfect. Being less than perfect, we need to learn to work in less-than-perfect environments with less-than-perfect people. It might even be that we will eventually discover that we can do wonders, even when we are not wonderful.

The secret to ministry is that we each have something to do. It may not be at all like someone else's work. It may not require the same frame of mind, the same skills, the same intelligence, or even the same behaviors. But it does require that it be the Lord's work. And since it is the Lord's work, we are under an obligation to observe the proclamation of Paul in Romans 14:4: "Who are you to judge the servants of someone else?" God can use such a variety of people and personalities, in such a variety of places and ways, that it would be impossible for us to judge the value of any other's offering until we have attained that perfect life ourselves—which is unlikely to happen until we are all resident in eternal glory.

The fervor for moral rightness has one small area of possible danger: Sometimes we become so convinced of our own interpretations and actions that we are not open to alternative perspectives, and we condemn others for crimes less than our own. We "strain at a gnat, and swallow a camel" (Matthew 23:24, King James Version). History is full of instances. Some of the most outwardly righteous people in our country practiced slavery with no twinge of conscience. One of the great financial swindlers of the twentieth century would not allow boys and girls to swim at the same time in his pool, for moral reasons, but he stole millions of dollars without a qualm. Think up your own examples.

Now think of the opposite, the great reformers. They were nearly all rejected by some people in their own time. John Wesley was banned from preaching in the Anglican churches because he dared assert that people are free to choose God and have an obligation to do responsible social action. Roger Williams, one of the founders of the Baptist Church in American, was driven from the Massachusetts Bay Colony because he believed in the separation of church and state and the rights of Native Americans to own their own land. But each of these, and hundreds of others, made a great contribution to the spiritual life of the country.

So, reformers are banished and scoundrels are admired because morality is not the same in all times, or always the same in all minds. That is why Paul, following Jesus' lead, spoke so often about tolerance and forgiveness. Some normally devout people are caught in moral and ethical lapses, and the actions and opinions of some outcasts may well be the cutting edge of a new spiritual direction. Patience is a requirement for all Christians and, indeed, for all of us.

A Spiritual Exercise: Intolerance in Our Day

While everyone has a different view of what is orthodox and what is heretical, we all have some opinion about who is intolerant and who is a person of moral conviction. Just for fun, make a list of groups or people whom you consider intolerant in our day. Give a reason for your choice.

What did you discover about yourself in this process?

Talk with others in your group.
What did you discover about others? Are we being fair?

Sometimes the dividing line between a defender of the faith and a bigot is narrow. Being virtuous is not only maintaining a healthy attitude to the standards of behavior that befit the Christian lifestyle but also maintaining a healthy attitude toward differences as to what constitutes true morality. Sometimes virtue comes down to a willingness to accept people, and ourselves, as works in progress and to wait to see what God will finally reveal to us about eternal values.

Meanwhile, the work of God goes on. In that arena also we have less than perfect insight. Sometimes what may seem like promising directions lead nowhere, and the least auspicious plans produce magnificent results. As much as we may want to do God's work, we may miss the call; and some that seem to have no purpose discover the way to fulfillment. God is always calling, but we are not always listening. Still, doing ministry is a path to spiritual achievement. We must keep on keeping on.

Submit to One Another

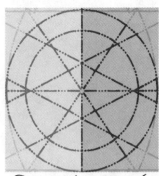

Many versions of the Bible use their own section headings, which may influence our understanding in a major way, even though the headings are not part of the Scripture itself. For instance, the *Good News Bible: Today's English Version* uses the heading "Wives and Husbands" for Ephesians 5:21-33. The King James Version names it "Of Husbands and Wives." The New Revised Standard Version calls this section "The Christian Household" (the only one even close to the actual meaning). The New International Version places today's text (Ephesians 5:2) in the previous section, separating it from its context, and calls Ephesians 5:22-33 "Wives and Husbands." Clearly, some of these heading avoid facing up to the actual meaning of the text, which clearly says "submit yourselves *to one another*" (emphasis added). Following that command are examples of how that works: with husbands and wives, with parents and children, and with slaves and masters. Each section is to be understood in terms of the general introductory statement, "Submit yourselves to one another."

The matter of submission has been a puzzle to Christians. Clearly, submission is a Christian virtue, but we have differences of opinion about who should submit to whom. And for reasons that are hard to fathom, it has usually been women who have suffered the consequence, in spite of the fact that the positive influence of women on the spiritual life is everywhere admired. Their submission may result from the fact that we have misunderstood the purpose of some biblical texts, one of which is today's lesson. Or it may be that men have traditionally believed women to be inferior and have grasped every opportunity to put them down.

> *Submit yourselves to one another because of your reverence for Christ.*
>
> (EPHESIANS 5:21)

We must deal with this statement about submitting by itself before we attempt to understand what follows. "Submit yourselves to one another" may be one of the most profound statements ever made. It means at least three things:

1. All power in the Body belongs to Christ alone, and it is shared equally with all the members of the Body. We do not owe subservience to any human.

2. The gifts are distributed to all, and their exercise is for the good of all. No one can claim credit for the results of the exercise of any gift. Therefore, no person should be exalted, nor any person debased, because of position or skills.

3. The Christian fellowship has no hierarchies. Everyone is submissive to everyone else. On any given day a person may be seen in obvious leadership positions, but on the next day someone else's gifts will be in the ascendency, and yesterday's leader may become today's follower. That is what submitting to one another means.

The idea of mutual subjection to one another is a primary component of Christian social relations. It is the opposite of self-assertion, exhibitionism, and the insistence on getting our own way. It expresses the essential character of the Christian as stated in Paul's letter to the Philippians: "Don't do anything from selfish ambition or from a cheap desire to boast, but be humble toward one another, always considering others better than yourselves. And look out for one another's interests, not just for your own" (Philippians 2:3-4).

The human desire for honor and dominance, though, are constantly at odds with God's divine plan. Gifted people often tend to want to lord it over those they consider less well endowed. Paul, informed by God, shows concern about this human condition as soon as the matter of the gifts is introduced. Paul warns Christians against becoming too proud of their aptitudes. In 1 Corinthians, he makes this point quickly: "Now remember what you were, my friends, when God called you. From the human point of view, few of you were wise or powerful or of high social standing. God purposely chose what the world considers nonsense in order to shame the wise, and he chose what the world considers weak to shame the powerful…. This means that no one can boast in God's presence" (1 Corinthians 1:26-27, 29).

Later in the same letter Paul remarks, "God himself has put the body together in such a way as to give greater honor to those parts that need it. And so there is no division in the body, but all its different parts have the same concern for one another. If one part of the body suffers, all the other parts suffer with it; if one part is praised, all the other parts share its happiness" (1 Corinthians 12:24-26).

In the second letter to the Corinthians, Paul speaks even more bluntly: "We who have this spiritual treasure are like common clay pots, in order to show that the supreme power belongs to God, not to us" (2 Corinthians 4:7). Since we are all alike, we are each empowered to do only God's work, and none of us can claim any power of his or her own. So, we are to submit to one another, each in turn as the power of the gifts spreads itself abroad. There are no slaves and no masters, except that we are all slaves of Christ and of one another. All this is done in "reverence for Christ" (Ephesians 5:21).

A Spiritual Exercise: Getting Even

List some of the things you can do in your church to show that we are all spiritually even with one another. How can we demonstrate that we are all gifted, but that no one's gifts are more important than another's?

Now arrange the ideas of your list in a paragraph or two that could serve as a covenant among you as a group, or the members of the church, in practicing your gifts of ministry.

Sign the covenant and show it to others.

In Romans 12, Paul explains that the gifts actually replace sacrifices as the offering of Christians: "Offer yourselves as a living sacrifice to God, dedicated to his service and pleasing to him. This is the true worship that you should offer" (Romans 12:1). Almost immediately he adds, "Because of God's gracious gift to me I say to every one of you: Do not think of yourself more highly than you should" (Romans 12:3). Then he repeats his definition of the Body so that they will not miss the connection: "We have many parts in the one body, and all these parts have different functions" (Romans 12:4). Being different is good, but bragging about it is self-serving, not God's service.

Our submission to one another, in the home or in society, is a way of recognizing the sole authority of God and placing our ministry in the context of true servanthood.

> *Put on God's armor now! Then when the evil day comes, you will be able to resist the enemy's attacks; and after fighting to the end, you will still hold your ground.*
>
> (EPHESIANS 6:13)

A Spiritual Exercise: God's Armor

Read Ephesians 6:10-20.
As you read, make a list of the elements of the armor that Paul recommends as a protection against the forces that would prevent our use of the gifts for ministry and the achievement of personal spirituality.

As a warning of the nature of the enemy, write beside each element of the armor its opposite, which would be the force against which it protects. (Individuals will have differences in what they consider the opposites to be.)

Armor

Protects Against

Discuss: From where do these forces come?

Preparing for ministry always includes developing spiritually. It is not enough to have gifts, to learn skills, to discover good methods, to be enthusiastic and hard-working. The fundamental resource for ministry is a right relationship with God. Paul says, "Build up your strength in union with the Lord and by means of his mighty power" (Ephesians 6:10).

Such a union involves the whole armor of God. Paul mentions a list of qualities that are part of the armor. All of these, together with a daily walk in the light of God's presence, make up the resources for ministry that surround the Christian. With that armor to protect us against the forces of distraction and destruction, we may learn and exercise the skills of ministry. In spite of the power of the Spirit, and of our own dedication to the work of God, the world and its forces press insistently on us. Maintaining the integrity of our use of the gifts for ministry is dependent on our ability to place the power of God between us and the outer and inner world in which we must practice our ministry of the gifts.

You are ready now to consider Parts 2 and 3 in this book. They give guidance for discovering, developing, and deploying your gifts. These actions can be a solitary, personal experience, or they may be part of your local church's planned ministry. If you have studied the Scripture as a group, you may want to study the remainder of the book as a group.

Spiritual Exercise: My Shield of Faith

Write the following in the four parts of the shield below:

1. Some words that identify sources of strength among your family of believers
2. Some words that describe your present personal faith
3. A phrase that describes something you do on behalf of Christ
4. A sentence that expresses your spiritual hope(s) for the future

If you are in a group, talk with one another about some parts of the shield.

Then let each person give a witness in exactly three words, such as "God is great" or "Jesus is Lord."

When all who wish to have witnessed, close with prayer.

Part 2

Spirituality and Practicality

Gifts are only a sidelight on the faith unless they are put to work in the community of believers and in the world around it. We can spend much time talking about gifts, worrying about whether we have them and which ones, and drawing up lists and taking tests; but it is all just an intellectual exercise unless the gifts are put to use. We sometimes think we can settle the issue with a weekend retreat and the analysis of a few test results, but the gifts of ministry are both more complex and more simple than that.

The gifts of ministry are more complex because we cannot merely construct a list of gifts from the information in the New Testament, assign people to each gift on the basis of tests or observation, and expect the whole work of the body of Christ to get done. While I have seen some masterful checklists and some interesting gift discovery tests devised by book writers and church councils, I have never seen one that contains all the skills and abilities that may be needed to do God's work in the world.

The gifts of ministry are more simple because many people who reflect on the gifts recognize what they have to offer in ministry, or simply do it without self-awareness. Others expect that they will know when the time is right and are not anxious about it. Add to that the call to ministry, which is God's way of activating gifts at appropriate times, and many people will find their way into ministry, even if no strategy is followed by the church—although a strategy can be helpful.

The significant point is that *all gifts and all calls are supremely personal.* God communicates with an individual concerning needs for ministry and the person's use of individual gifts in response. While participation in planning for the work of the Christian community may broaden our understanding of ministry and provide a supportive atmosphere in which to practice it, every person's gifts are ultimately related to the presence of God in individual lives and become effective only in the context of a closer walk with God—what we call spirituality. Remember, it was Paul's answer in 1 Corinthians 12 to the question "What is spirituality [*pneumatikos*]?" that led to the identification of the gifts as the source of Christian ministry. Spirituality releases the gifts, and the gifts expand spirituality.

Since I have come to believe that the local church must focus on spirituality in order to revitalize the Body, I think we must come to terms with the meaning of spirituality and help our constituents focus on it in their own lives and in every area of the life of the church.

The formation of so many Christian groups (by some counts, as many as 1,200 denominations, as well as many independent churches) has produced a profusion of definitions of spirituality. On page 36 there are ten characteristic ones. As you read each definition, write in the name of any religious groups or individuals who are identified with each perspective, or with a combination of them. Do you see your own spirituality described in any of these?

1. *A regimen of prayer, meditation, and disciplined study*—Brought to flower in the monastic movement, this definition is sometimes called spiritual formation.
(*Group or person*): _____

2. *A verbal/vocal expression of joy*—I grew up in a "shouting" Methodist church. My home church has long since become more subdued. Others, though, still stress a demonstrative style as evidence of the presence of the Holy Spirit, which for some is the only proof of spirituality.
(*Group or person*): _____

3. *An emphasis on personal, moral, and emotional purity,* sometimes called holiness—Much emphasis is placed on the contrast between the flesh and the spirit. Worldliness is condemned, sometimes in forms that others find acceptable (such as seeing movies, playing card games, dancing, or driving cars). Rigid behavioral regulations are set for all, and the level of spirituality is judged by how well each one meets these requirements.
(*Group or person*): _____

4. *Mystical experience*—Visions, dreams, and insights are valued as evidence of spirituality. They range from a cultivation of the universal spirit to specific predictive visions of the present or future (sometimes called prophecy). Both Christian and non-Christian religious leaders have prized this experience.
(*Group or person*): _____

5. *Sacramental practice*—The Mass (Holy Communion), baptism, penance, sacrifice (giving or giving up things), and the observance of other liturgies and rituals have been considered a source of spirituality for as long as religious history records.
(*Group or person*): _____

6. *The activist mode*—For some, there is no spirituality unless evidenced in acts of love, mercy, and justice. The practices of Christian social responsibility are drawn from the New Testament in the words and actions of Jesus (for example, the story of the Last Judgment in Matthew 25:31-46), the Letter of James, and other New Testament sources.
(*Group or person*): _____

7. *Apocalyptic preparation*—Christian living is defined as discerning the pattern of history and preparing for the end. Spirituality is moving toward the rapture (not a biblical word).
(*Group or person*): _____

8. *Doctrinal purity* (right beliefs)—The basis of orthodoxy, this perspective emphasizes the setting of approved beliefs that everyone must subscribe to as a basis for spiritual growth. From the beginning, the church has had groups who have set up such tenets (calling them basic or fundamental beliefs), although specifics have varied from age to age.
(*Group or person*): _____

9. *Evidences of miracles, signs, and wonders*—The test of the vitality of individuals and churches is whether they can produce supernatural phenomena. Dispensationalists insist that the miracles of the Bible were real, but that such experiences stopped with apostolic times. Others think that strong faith still produces supernatural results.
(*Group or person*): _____

10. *Unique theologies*—Some individualistic theologies, developed by charismatic individuals or dedicated groups, define spirituality as embodying the expression of faith originated by the person or group. These groups are often called sects at their beginning, but some go on to join the mainstream.
(*Group or person*): _____

Have you observed evidence of other definitions of spirituality in your own church or community? If so, write a definition to describe what you have observed. Name a group or person for each one.

Definition: _____
_____
_____

Person or Group: _____

Definition: _____
_____
_____

Person or Group: _____

Question: Which of these expresses the essence of spirituality?
Answer: All of them, and none of them!

Diligent reading can find most of theses viewpoints in the New Testament. Even a cursory review of church history will reveal that at various stages every one of them, along with many others, has been stressed by someone. In his writings, Paul acknowledges that he has spoken in tongues (1 Corinthians 14:18), has seen visions (2 Corinthians 12:1), and has done miracles and wonders (Romans 15:17-19; 2 Corinthians 12:12). However, he insists that these signs are not the only expressions of spirituality. He even explains that the Lord has given him a painful physical ailment to keep him from bragging about any of these (2 Corinthians 12:7). In 1 Corinthians 13, Paul says that any spiritual expression or ministry must take place in the context of love. Clearly, Paul understood that God recognizes the need for diversity in spiritual experiences.

Any spiritual experience may be helpful, but none are exclusive of all others. Why did God allow that to happen? *Perhaps it was because God knew that things would change over time for believers.* For fourteen hundred years, almost all Christians worshiped through the Mass, or liturgies based on it; but that has changed since the Reformation. Groups have developed their own ways of worship and spiritual growth. Often, people are trained to value a specific perspective on spirituality by their denominations, congregations, or parents. Some may come to think that any other variety of religious expression is invalid. When the mobility of modern society or community changes, or interdenominational marriage brings them into the company of others who experience other styles of worship and practice, they sometimes feel uneasy. Could it be that God led denominations to establish traditions that were similar from place to place so that members could go from one church to another with confidence, and then prompted many local churches in our time to develop multiple styles to accommodate the needs of those from different traditions? We are still struggling with all that.

Perhaps God allowed such diversity in spiritual experiences because God has made people naturally different. Each specific mixture of genetics and experience that makes up personality carries a characteristic set of both physical and spiritual hungers. Distinctive expressions of spirituality are required to accommodate these differences. Paul spoke of being "all things to all people" so that some may be saved (1 Corinthians 9:22). God is still opening the vision of disciples in developing responses to this multiplicity of needs.

Perhaps there is diversity in spiritual experiences because people are gifted in different ways. Spiritual experience is part of the preparation for doing God's work. Since the gifts are varied, spiritual experiences must be varied as well. Perhaps God planned for people to have a variety of worship and spiritual-growth experiences because there are different requirements for equipping people to do the ministries to which they feel called and gifted.

In any case, there are many needs and many expressions. How do we keep that from being a bewildering experience for the church and a distraction in equipping God's people for ministry?

The title of this book, *Each One a Minister,* implies that ministry is first an individual experience, with both the gifts and the call coming through the grace of God. The preparation for ministry is also distinctive, with each person being equipped in a different way, depending on the temperament of the individual and the nature of the call. While there are times for corporate discernment and organizational goals and emphases, there is always a time for the individual who feels a distinct call from God and seeks fresh avenues and uncharted arenas of service. The history of Christianity has been formed by such people.
When spiritual lives are charged, people hear God's call.

The Role and Practice of Spirituality

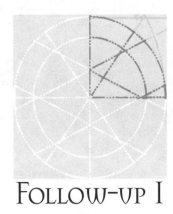

Cultivating the Spiritual

Are there ways to encourage spiritual growth in ourselves and in our friends in Christ, even though we are all so different? While some church fellowships seem more spiritually enthused than others, and some attain a general consensus on types of spiritual-growth activities that are helpful, there are few that provide all the people of the Body with all the spiritual resources they need. The number of people who move from one denomination or church to another, or simply drop out altogether, is evidence that all spiritual lives are not sustained by the same elements.

It may be that the premise that everyone must participate in the same public worship and spiritual-growth experiences is itself faulty. Many local churches judge loyalty to God by the frequency of attendance at traditional morning worship and participation in the official program of the congregation. For many years, most members of local churches have felt obligated to do what others are doing in the church, whether it met their spiritual needs or not. For these people, the only solution to mismatches between individual needs and churchwide activities seemed to be to go to another church, or to none at all.

Must those who do not feel spiritually nourished by the program of the local church give up their own spiritual search or go somewhere else? Increasingly the answer is no. A considerable number of churches are offering choices in styles of worship, spiritual-growth opportunities, and ministry processes. Greater emphasis is being placed on the multiplicity of the gifts and the varieties of preparation for them. More and more individuals are discovering that their gifts can be employed in a church even if its dominant program themes are in areas where they do not feel a special call or interest. *All members do not have to do the same things in order to feel included or useful.* Spiritual lives can be enriched in ways that are compatible with individual needs.

In the church I attend (about 900 members), we have four different general worship opportunities. Two are on Sunday morning: an experience with a traditional liturgy, choirs, and a printed order of worship; and a contemporary service with an informal structure, praise choruses, and instrumental music. The Sunday evening service is brush-arbor style, with old favorite hymns and a variety of speakers. On Wednesday night there is a supper, with family fellowship and special worship and study. Some people come to the service that gives them the most spiritual support; others attend two or three. Few, if any, attend all of them.

We have various people involved in numerous Sunday school classes, each different in its approach, and in small-group spiritual-growth activities: DISCIPLE Bible study and other disciplined Bible and book study groups, prayer groups, spiritual discovery groups, choirs, women's circles, men's groups, youth groups, and special groups formed by those who have a specific interest in some area of Christian living. People start new groups from time to time to respond to expressed spiritual needs. (We used to discourage such innovations, but now we welcome them.) Again, no one attends all of these, or even a majority of them. Each person chooses the activity that will meet his or her spiritual needs. Nobody keeps score. People drop in and out as they feel the need. Some in the church attend only one of these (or none); others may be involved in many over the years.

Our church is not especially active, but it is typical. Many avenues of spiritual exploration are available; and if there is not one to suit your needs, you can start one. Just a few years ago that would have been unthinkable. At that time most churches had only one worship style and a few programs. Everyone was expected to participate in all the activities, whether his or her needs were met or not. While only a handful actually did so, the ones who did were judged to be the most pious and therefore entitled to control the spiritual life of the congregation. In some churches they did.

Now the trend is toward an emphasis on personal spirituality and ministry and a decrease in general program involvement. In many churches small ministry groups do most of the work, and the whole congregation gathers only for worship, study, and celebration. The council still seeks God's guidance for the whole church and plans and administers its organized program, but individuals and teams who feel called are encouraged to do their own ministry, in keeping with the theology and mission of the Body.

Some Suggestions for Extending Spirituality

- *Develop a rich and varied prayer life.* Whatever the type of public worship in the church, people can reach toward God in private moments. While public worship is a great asset to personal spiritual vitality, it is not a necessity for us to like the hymns or the order of worship, or even the pastor's sermons, in order to grow in spirit there. Prayer is the avenue to God's presence, and anyone can pray anytime. If our personal and family lives are filled with prayer, we need not worry about those in the church with whom we do not agree, or who do not agree with us, or even the secular world. Prayers in classrooms and at ball games and public events are only symbolic, but prayer in the heart and home is real. Some people find it meaningful to pray throughout the entire church worship service. For the person with an abundant prayer life, any church, any community, can be enriching.

- *Gather with others to pray, study, and talk about important issues.* Many of the large churches of the world focus on cell groups for their spiritual life. There people gather weekly in cells of from eight to ten members for encouragement from one another and for communion with God. Many churches use this Wesleyan model for the whole congregation. (*The Book of Discipline of The United Methodist Church—2000,* ¶¶ 255 and 255.1, strongly encourages the formation of such groups.) Anyone can get with friends for sharing spiritual experiences and needs. No permission is required and no professional leadership is necessary. Those who feel a need for more-spiritual resources in daily life or church settings can often find them in small groups. And, even more importantly, small-group environments are more likely to produce awareness of the gifts of ministry and to promote the practice of them.

One Warning: Such groups must guard against becoming exclusive or self-righteous. A satisfying personal experience does not give us cause for feeling or acting superior to others. Such gatherings are for the enhancement of our spiritual lives, and the methods we use may not be helpful to everyone. We cannot hold them to our standards or require them to do as we do.

- *Encourage the church to initiate types of worship experiences that serve the needs of various groups.* Laity can exercise great influence on the pattern of the worship life of the congregation if they approach it with sensitivity and tact. Pastors and other leaders are looking for new ideas all the time. All of us can help if we are willing to observe the disciplines and proprieties of successful change processes.

  — One nearby creative small congregation, encouraged by a United Methodist Hispanic couple, has initiated a second morning worship in Spanish, based on the traditional liturgy, to serve the growing number of Hispanic migrant workers in our area. They have responded.

  — Some people in one church I served were concerned that we had Holy Communion only once a quarter. Previous pastors had responded to the reduced attendance on Communion Sundays by reducing the number of Communion services. Under the guidance of those who were concerned, we turned a large room into a chapel and had our evening worship there, with the Lord's Supper served on the first Sunday evening of each month when we did not have it in the morning. Both Sunday morning and Sunday evening attendance increased.

  — Another medium-sized local church, in response to youth requests, has added a Saturday night celebration to its weekly worship offerings. Aimed at youth, it features Christian rock music and informal preaching and interaction. So far it is a great success.

  — At least two United Methodist churches in our area now have four morning worship services, each designed for a different audience. Some are held in the sanctuary, some in a fellowship hall, some in a chapel, and at least one in an empty commercial building nearby. Both the worship and the setting are designed to serve different needs.

Criticisms of present services or leaders, or pressure tactics, are not likely to work; but thoughtful, helpful analysis and discovery can do wonders. Privately or publicly, we can increase our spiritual strength through the development of compatible modes and methods for spiritual growth for ourselves and others in the public worship of our local churches.

Questions We Can Ask Ourselves

1. What would encourage our personal spiritual development the most?
2. What have we done for ourselves? What can we do?
3. How can we help our church meet more of the spiritual needs of people?

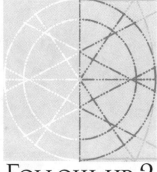

Discovering Gifts for Ministry

Remembering Ephesians 2:10, we should remind ourselves that the purpose for building up our spiritual life is to prepare to do ministry in the name of Jesus Christ, and the purpose for doing ministry is to build up our spiritual life. Spirituality releases the gifts, and the gifts expand spirituality.

Pursuing spirituality is not intended to provide us with an excuse for self-congratulation. Some of us take pleasure in "much speaking" (Matthew 6:7, King James Version) and cultivate reputations for personal piety and public visibility in Christian gatherings (like the Pharisees?). We often misconstrue *spiritual pride* as *spiritual power*. We do not heed Paul's warning not to "think of yourself more highly than you should" (Romans 12:3). However, within the Body, seeking spirituality is encouraged because it strengthens faith and facilitates the ministry of the gifts. The closer we are to God, the more likely it is that we will discover what God wants us to be and do.

The quest for discovering our gifts and ministry can be either individual or corporate (organizational). For some, the best plan is to seek God's call in private or with trusted friends, with prayer and personal search as the operative factors. For others, a large-group process with presentations, tests (instruments), churchwide needs, and group discussion may be the most helpful route. Over time both may be part of a comprehensive process of gifts discovery.

In this book, we will deal primarily with the personal dimensions of gifts discovery. A number of resources for churchwide assessments of not only spiritual gifts but also factors must be considered as we make decisions about deploying each person as a minister in a specific ministry. *Equipped for Every Good Work: Building a Gifts-Based Church,* by Dan R. Dick and Barbara Miller (Discipleship Resources, 2001), has tools for exploration of spiritual gifts, leadership and interaction styles, work style preferences, and spirituality types. Other resources for gifts exploration are listed in Part 4 in this book.

> God has made us what we are, and in our union with Christ Jesus he has created us for a life of good deeds, which he has already prepared for us to do.
>
> (EPHESIANS 2:10)

Theological Foundations

As with any other Christian quest, our methodology will depend heavily on our theology. I would like to suggest that there is a perspective on the gifts for ministry that encourages us to search for and practice them. That perspective also frees us from stereotypes that have often interfered with our enjoyment of the Christian community. Here are some facets of that view, based on our previous study of Ephesians. It could be called a biblical theology of the gifts.

Spirituality releases the gifts, and the gifts expand spirituality.

1. *The gifts are intrinsic to (a basic part of) the plan of salvation.* They precede from the same source as does justification. We are saved by grace and gifted by grace, a seamless whole.

2. *The purpose of the gifts is to do ministry.* The gifts are not for personal enhancement or a cause for feeling superior. They are practical talents, skills, and

resources for doing God's work, which are acquired or focused and made more powerful through the presence of God in our lives.

3. *The gifts are not mysterious or exotic.* No special spiritual achievement or leadership position is required for their application. While some expressions of gifts may be amazing, and the results far beyond normal expectations, they are not supernatural. They are a normal part of the plan of God for all people who love God and want to serve God.

4. *All the gifts are equal in value.* While some gifts may be publicly admired more than others, and some may bring uncommon results, the actual value to the realm of faith is the same for all. God has set them in place, and each is dependent on all the others. The least impressive gift may be the key for the achievement of God's purpose.

5. *No single gift or set of gifts can be used as a test of Christian achievement or commitment.* Some sects have claimed that speaking in tongues, doing miracles, or having some other special gift must be present in order to prove that a person or a church is truly spiritual. While all Christians are gifted, we can neither know nor enforce any such hierarchy of values. We are each a full minister of Christ and a full member of the Body.

6. *The call to use the gifts is not necessarily dramatic or difficult.* While some have been suddenly awakened to God's call and have responded splendidly, most discover the call of God on their lives within the course of a normal Christian life experience. In some cases, the practice of the ministry will even precede the discovery of the gift (see Part 3). Some people may be in ministry for a while before they realize that they have been exercising their gifts all along. Some may be just doing what comes naturally, in a spiritual sense.

7. *The discovery of our gifts will not always bring us immediate happiness and gratification.* We are constantly warned that God's call is occasionally painful and dangerous. Sometimes we do not even want to know what God is calling us to do; and when we do know God is calling, we are tempted to decline the offer. Stories of such experiences abound in Christian literature. But we are assured of eternal values and personal fulfillment. Realization of the gifts ultimately brings contentment.

8. *We may never recognize the nature of our gifts or think that we fully know the will of God.* However, we are still part of God's plan and can expect to receive reassurance of God's blessings and final vindication. God does not abandon those who earnestly seek to serve.

9. *The gifts are not limited to, nor defined by, those listed in 1 Corinthians 12; Romans 12; or Ephesians 4.* Others are mentioned in the New Testament: peacemaking, caregiving, hospitality, intercession, community building, and so forth. And even more are apparent in the world of believers. God's gifts are as varied as God's people, and differences among the talents of servants of Christ increase the power of all. Paraphrasing Paul: If we were all alike, there would not be a body.

10. *The search for the gifts and the call of God is worthwhile, whatever the outcome.* As long as we believe that God rules, we are never without hope and meaning. As long as we can serve God's people, we are doing the work of God, whether we give it a particular name or not.

Discovering Gifts of Ministry

Apart from participating in the planning processes of the local church, what can we do to claim and use our gifts? Between theoretical and practical, the practical is the most difficult. But we must eventually get practical if the gifts are to mean anything to us or to the Body. What are some reasonable and prudent steps we can take to find our place in God's economy?

■ *Spiritual preparation*—We have already discussed spiritual preparation at length, but we need to be reminded that spirituality is not an occasional experience; it is a lifestyle. Each day is a new beginning, and prayer and reflection are never out of style.

■ *Definition*—In solitude, or in a small group, we can decide what we mean by gifts. Are the gifts for ministry limited to the biblical lists, or are they expressions of the values and qualities that God needs in every age to do God's work? While a majority of the books on gifts deal mostly with the New Testament names, many of them also acknowledge that the definition of giftedness goes well beyond those attributes. To spend some time examining that concept, look at the composite list below. Check the ones you think could be gifts.

❑ Caregiving	❑ Financial Management	❑ Mediating
❑ Evaluating		❑ Insight
❑ Managing	❑ Music	❑ Decorating
❑ Maintenance	❑ Constructing	❑ Supervising
❑ Counseling	❑ Writing	❑ Waitering
❑ Teaching	❑ Speaking	❑ Selling
❑ Helping	❑ Rationality	❑ Interpreting
❑ Stewardship	❑ Supporting	❑ Compassion
❑ Designing	❑ Policing	❑ Other _____
❑ Witnessing	❑ Cleaning	❑ Other _____

This list is intended to demonstrate four facets of gifts:

1. Gifts are as varied as our descriptive ability and may include anything we can identify.
2. Gifts are not confined to church settings, but are for serving in the world also.
3. Gifts are not always imposing, but may also include the common tasks of life.
4. God is in the details as well as in the whole of existence.

Do you agree with any or all of the above statements? Do they help or hinder the search for your gifts? How would you modify them to fit your perceptions?

■ *Self-examination*—Using whatever definition you have reached for the gifts, spend some time examining your own feelings about ministry and where you might fit into God's plan. This is a point at which a small group of trusted fellow Christians might be especially helpful.

Use your own process, but if you have difficulty getting started, you might try asking yourself these questions:

• What have I sometimes thought I am particularly prepared to do?
• What has happened when I have tried to practice this skill or ability?

- Have I felt a sense of rightness about this area of my life?
- What are some of the other areas of service or ministry to which I have been drawn?
- What has caused me to be interested in those areas?
- Do any of them give me a sense of being called or chosen?

Then write your answers to these two questions:
- What possible gifts can I claim? _____
_____

- What ministry can I do that will express this gift (these gifts)?

_____

_____

If you are still in a quandary, read the following:

One of the most frequently asked questions among Christians who are aware of the gifts process is, "Why can't I recognize what gifts I have right now?" The answer to that inquiry has two levels. The first is that discovering gifts is like any other search process—the right conditions have to be present to succeed. There is a fullness of time. At any given time, we may
- not have all the information we need about the process;
- lack self-understanding;
- be in a less intensive state of spiritual awareness;
- need more motivation;
- be engaged in other important Christian activities;
- have life crises that prevent us from focusing on ministry.

The list could continue indefinitely. While the search for gifts is a lifelong vocation, it does not necessarily lead to enlightenment immediately. We need not be overly concerned if we are unable to discover our area of giftedness at any specific moment. I heard a man in Raleigh, North Carolina, say, "I have spent all my life wondering what gift I had; and since I have retired, I think I have finally found it." On the other hand, a young woman in Atlanta said, "Ever since childhood I have been able to bring together people who have differences. That gift has shaped my life." A man somewhere else said, "I seem to have different gifts every few years of my life. Why is that?" (Perhaps he had the gift of adaptability. We could all use that one.) The thing to remember is that there are different stages of readiness.

The second level of the answer is that the environment for ministry may not always be present. Circumstances can alter opportunities. We may
- live in a setting where our gifts are not needed at this time;
- be in a dysfunctional church, or a dysfunctional period in our own life;
- lack the support and encouragement that makes discovery possible.

When Paul began preaching after his conversion on the Damascus Road, the reaction was so negative that he was sent back to Tarsus for a long period of time (Acts 9:30). He did not return to his ministry until a number of years later, when Barnabas invited him to help at Antioch. He was a different person by that time, and God was able to use him mightily. The inability to serve at one time in our lives does not prevent us from trying again, and succeeding. We may have to wait for our search for the gifts to be successful, but we do not have to wait to serve God.

■ *Discernment*—The discovery of our gifts is more a matter of discernment than of investigation. Discernment is discovering the will of God for our lives. Ultimately, the question is not "What can I do best?" but "What does God want me to do?" So, discovering our gifts is a spiritual exercise rather than an analysis of our skills and abilities. The gifts, the ministry, and the setting are all intertwined. We may find clues to God's will for us in any of them if we are willing to look.

Gift is the key to finding God's will for people who discover an inclination to use a special quality in their lives on behalf of the work of God. They recognize a personal skill or talent that gives them purpose and passion and provides them with a sense of mission. For a time, or for the rest of their lives, they are inspired by that vision and guided toward its fulfillment wherever that takes them. They look for ministries and settings in which the gift may be practiced. A local church staff member in a nearby community told me that he had been a successful manager in a factory for twenty years and had always thought that he ought to be able to use that skill for the church. When he retired, his own local church was seeking an administrator, so he applied. Now he feels even more fulfilled.

Ministry is the driving force for some people. Seeing the needs around them, or being introduced to an area of special promise, they will discover themselves responding by evoking hitherto unrecognized abilities that become tools for that ministry. As the ministry changes, they may discover new gifts that can keep them related to it. Some years ago, some friends of ours who had never taken a big interest in local church programs were introduced to an agency that relocated refugee families from Vietnam to the United States. They became deeply involved, and the whole agency was strengthened by their gifts and passion for the task. When the agency closed after its task was completed, the couple went on to another similar ministry.

Setting is the key for other people. Some people may drift spiritually for much of their life and then suddenly find themselves in an environment where everything comes into focus. While I served a medium-sized church in a large city, I had a call from a pastor of a smaller congregation in a distant community who said he wanted to thank us for sending them a new couple. He said that their whole church was being revitalized by the presence and actions of these new members, who had come from our church. I was astonished. I had known the couple only barely, because they were not involved in our church at all beyond attendance at morning worship. Neither of them had ever served on a committee or been an officer of the church, or even come to Sunday school. But in this new church their gifts were changing everything.

When the couple came back for a family visit, I had a chance to talk to them. I told them about the phone call, trying to hide my surprised reaction. But they sensed it anyway. They offered this comment, "While we were here, everything appeared to be running fine. The leaders were doing a good job, and the people seemed interested and involved. But when we got to that church, it was so apathetic and unfocused that we couldn't stand it any longer. We decided that it needed our gifts, so we went to work."

In the final analysis, discovering gifts is a product of keeping our spirits open to the call of God. The indwelling Christ reveals us to ourselves in various settings and through varied ministries. Sometimes when we are looking, and at other times when we are least aware, we discern the call of God and our gifts and how they fit together.

■ *Volunteering*—The local church must discover its own mission and ministry through a process of discernment and planning by the board or council. Once the ministry has been discerned, it is time for planning. Planning includes the development of an organization and procedures to do the ministry. Various committees and teams may be formed, along with paid or unpaid personnel to accomplish the mission. Some of the personnel in larger churches may be professionals, hired to do some tasks because of their giftedness. Most often, though, the personnel is laity, drawn to the work of the church and willing to help where they can. These are the volunteers, doing the work outlined by church organizations or leaders. They may answer phones, help with mailings, serve church suppers, visit the sick, prepare meeting places, serve on teams and committees, lead Sunday school classes or small groups, greet worshipers, contact people who may be interested in attending church, organize prayer groups, or dozens of other tasks—all in support of the mission and ministry of the local church. Without these volunteers, where would we be?

> **Ministry comes first; organization follows.**

We have used the term *volunteer* for many years to describe people who help organizations do church and community service. *Volunteer* is still a valid term. Volunteers are needed to do the everyday tasks of the church and world, even if they have not identified their own unique gifts. For some, this can be the first step in the discovery of their own ministry.

When we speak of being in ministry, we mean more than just being a volunteer, though. Ministry is a vocation derived from our gifts, a response to the call of God, the acceptance of a role in the work of God. Laity are called to ministry, just as clergy are called. Unless laity assume their full share of responsibility for building the Body, the church will always be deficient. For the church to fully realize its whole ministry, it must incorporate many people who have discovered their gifts, have developed them, and are willing to practice them in appropriate settings, even if the settings have not been planned by the church council. The church is built on these gifts for ministry.

A major responsibility of the church is to encourage and assimilate the gifts of its members. As I said earlier, the church is the sum of the gifts of its members. Some people complain that many members do not participate in the work of the church. Could it be that we have developed a program that pleases the core members, who are probably doing the complaining, and overlook those who are being called to use gifts and do ministries that are not on our official list? Maybe so. However, many of us want to do something but are unsure of our call. Being a part of the volunteer corps can be a marvelous way to get started. For some, that service may lead to a called ministry or may become a ministry in itself.

I would not want to leave the impression that the search for the gifts is useless or that church programs to encourage gifts discovery are a waste. Far from it. The emphasis on the gifts for ministry is not always understood, and every effort to involve people in learning experiences is worthwhile. Many people dismiss the gifts as an aberration of the charismatics, which does not deserve serious consideration by mainline Christians. The church must counter that impression with a thoughtful explanation and presentation of gifts theology and an exploration of the gifts as a source of ministry formation. The gifts discovery weekends and other offerings by the local church are invaluable in giving gifts discovery credibility and legitimacy.

A Personal Plan for Gifts Discovery

1. Maintain spirituality.
2. Study Scripture and other resources (see the list of resources in Part 4).
3. If possible, join with some trusted friends who are also searching.
4. Attend a gifts discovery workshop in your church or town, or use one or more of the many gifts discovery inventories to get ideas. The following are useful:
   - *Equipped for Every Good Work: Building a Gifts-Based Church,* by Dan R. Dick and Barbara Miller (Discipleship Resources, 2001), pages 31–36. (This book also includes tools for helping you discover your leadership and interaction styles, your work style preferences, and your spirituality type. All of these things together can help you and the members of your congregation discover your places of ministry in your church and community.
   - *Rediscovering Our Spiritual Gifts,* by Charles V. Bryant (Upper Room, 1991), pages 155-76.
   - *Network: Understanding God's Design for You in the Church* (participant's guide, leader's guide, or both), by Bruce Bugbee, Don Cousins, and Bill Hybels (Zondervan, 1994).

   Remember, these inventories may not bring you to conclusions, but they can lead to beginnings. While you may not reach decisions about your own gifts, you will learn more about the concept of gifts in general.
5. Be on the lookout for signs and sources of gifts confirmation:
   - a sense of God's call to use a specific skill or quality;
   - a persistent feeling of identification with a special area of ministry;
   - a feeling of rightness about decisions and directions;
   - affirmations of visible gifts or qualities by other people;
   - an impression of summons or challenge.
6. Consider the whole area of gifts, ministries, and settings. Examine the ministries outlined in Part 3 in this book. Identify the direction that provides you with the most insight. Do not forget that ministries do not have to be churchy. Then answer these questions:
   - If *gifts* is the basis for your attraction to an area: What ministry would use them best? Where can I invest my spiritual energies?
   - If *ministries* is the basis for your attraction to an area: What gifts will be needed? Where are these satisfying ministries available?
   - If *settings* is the basis for your attraction to an area: What ministries will apply? How can my gifts be adapted?
7. When you are ready, choose a tentative identification of gift, ministry, or setting. Tell your friends, your pastor, and/or the church coordinator of small-group ministries. Ask them for reactions. Let their comments clarify your vision.
8. If you feel a call to a definite direction, try to describe it as accurately as possible. Then develop plans to create the conditions under which the call can become a reality. Ask yourself these questions:
   - Am I clear about the nature of my gift(s)?
   - Do I feel a call to use my gift in a general way, or in a specific ministry?
   - Am I passionate about these areas of ministry and eager to become involved?
9. If you do not arrive at a conclusion right away, continue to pray and wait for time to bring insight. Remember all you know about the importance of living in God's time rather than in your own.

After thirty-three happy years serving as a pastor and district superintendent, I heard of a new position being proposed for our Conference Council on Ministries staff in leader development and continuing education. Having felt drawn to that ministry for many years, and receiving many affirmations when I attempted service in that area, I felt called to apply for the position. I was chosen and I accepted, although at a considerable loss of salary. The next nine years brought me the most fulfillment of all my time in ministry. It seemed that God had been calling me to that ministry all my professional life, but it took a particular set of circumstances for it to become reality.

When you have made a decision, or feel the need of a more-intense involvement in the search, fill out this form; then take it to your pastor or coordinator of ministries.

I feel a call to support the ministries of the church and would like to offer my services in the following area(s):

_____

_____

I think I have gifts to offer the community of faith and would like an opportunity to put them into practice. My gifts are the following:

_____

_____

I feel called to develop a ministry in/for _____ and would like to have support in developing a ministry plan and/or team.

I have a call to ministry as a layperson, but I am not sure which ministries would be best for me. I would like to be in a group to explore gifts and ministries.

_____

Signed

Phone: _____ E-mail: _____

Mailing Address: _____

_____

If your church has a similar form, by all means use it. If it does not, suggest that it develop one and distribute it to all members. One way to distribute the form is to include it in the bulletin once a month or to have copies in the pew racks on a regular basis.

Continue to encourage the church to stress gifts and to provide resources for those who want to discover them. You may be the key to the process of awakening the church to its task as an administrator of the gifts for ministry that God has given the people in your church.

Not all local church ministry is known to everyone. Many people and groups who are called are doing ministries that others do not see and that are never listed in the program of the church council. Some people are not aware that what they are doing is a ministry of the gifts. Ask for a ministry audit in your church, where every ministry being done by anyone is put on a list, and perhaps published. It might be an eye opener for many. Your church may be doing a lot more than you thought, and it will encourage laity to use their gifts by affirming that every ministry is vital to the life of the church and to the life of faith.

Developing and
Deploying the Gifts

Over the years I have heard hundreds of remarks such as these:

"I always knew that I had a calling. In the last year, I have found that it is caring for others. I now work as a full-time volunteer in a nursing home in the community, and I feel blessed."

"We had this big fight in the church a few years ago, and I found out that my friend Martha had the gift of peacemaking. Since then I have seen it in her many times."

"I don't see myself with a specific call right now, but I plan to stay open to God's voice."

"I finally agreed to help in Bible school one summer and realized that I was called to be a teacher. I have been happily teaching in public schools for fifteen years now."

"I never once thought about being in ministry myself (I thought that was for the preacher) until last year's gifts discovery weekend. Since then I have started a divorce recovery group. For the first time I feel useful and fulfilled."

"I guess my gift must be helping. I can't do much but answer the telephone and stuff envelopes in the church office. Does that count?" (The answer is yes.)

Development of Gifts

The study of Ephesians reminds us that even the gifted need equipping for ministry. We cannot always just jump right in. The development of our understanding and skills may take longer than the process of discovery. This subject has attracted a great deal of attention in recent years. If you read a list of books on ministry, you will find a number of them with some form of the word *equipping* in the title. Many authors/lecturers have even said that the role of the pastor in today's church is not to do ministry but to equip people for ministry. Since few of us have been trained to equip others, we do not attempt it regularly. Instead, we just assign people to tasks, with no training or support, and then wonder why they feel uncomfortable and back out or become inactive within a short time.

Pastors, Christian educators, and other professionals often spend years learning their ministries. Is there any reason to think that laity suddenly become proficient even if their enthusiasm is high? Certainly not in every case. Some of us are called because we are equipped, but some of us are called with much equipping still to be done. The development of the ability to minister may be a major factor in doing it well.

Gifts are the raw material of ministry. Because they are so personal and compelling, it is tempting to believe that gifts are sufficient in themselves. Just as some new local pastors feel resentful of the standards of ministry they must meet in order to be ordained, so some laypeople believe that their fervor is more than enough to guarantee success in the application of gifts to ministry. But there are some considerations:

1. *Many ministries need special skills that can be learned through experiences or class sessions.* Caring for special needs of people may be more effective if we study or participate in learning opportunities about that ministry area. Witnessing may require an introduction to techniques and conditions. The United Methodist Church once had a national process for teaching ministry skills. These Christian enrichment schools prepared people for many roles within and outside of the church. While the enrichment schools are gone, the spirit lives on. We can find sources of learning in our own communities and denominational seminars.

2. *If others will be involved in the ministry, someone should be equipped to lead groups.* While some have natural skills, most need to learn the dynamics and flow of group life. Some helpful qualities for leaders include
   • an understanding of servant leadership, as defined by Jesus;
   • an experience of spirituality and an aptitude for encouraging it in others;
   • the ability to lead in team building and to encourage cooperation;
   • competency in structuring agendas and in expediting routine matters;
   • an ability to assess the mood of a group and to choose appropriate procedures to respond;
   • the capability to get people to interact without contention;
   • skills in processing issues and leading toward consensus decisions;
   • a knowledge of how to bring closure to issues and meetings, especially meetings.
   If you do not have these qualities, perhaps you should read a book on techniques or attend a session on group leadership. Communities and churches often sponsor such training. I highly recommend the book *The Christian Small-Group Leader,* by Thomas R. Hawkins (Discipleship Resources, 2001), and *Lay Speakers Lead Small Groups,* by Thomas R. Hawkins (Discipleship Resources, 2001), which is the Lay Speaker Advanced Course that uses *The Christian Small-Group Leader* as its text.

3. *Leaders need to learn the process of steering matters through organizations.* Many ministries falter before they gain momentum because people who feel the call fail to develop a strategy for implementing proposals.

Other areas of development may be needed. Significant change seldom occurs in organizations, of which the church is one, unless change agents develop the skills needed. Called people are usually change agents.

DEPLOYMENT OF GIFTED PEOPLE

The critical point in the gifts process is using the gifts for ministry in the local church or in the world at large. As I said before, this is not an intellectual exercise. Gifts discovery is not a way to fill time or to obtain self-gratification; it is a preparation for doing the work of God. It must be undertaken with care. It is the first step in a process that leads to development of our understanding and abilities and the deployment of our gifts in the actual places where they will best serve the cause of Christ.

While the world is our parish—and we must be willing to go wherever our gifts are needed—the first consideration might well be the relationship of our gifts to our local church:

- Is that the place where my gifts may best be employed?
- Are my gifts appropriate to the mission of my church at this time?
- How can I relate to the local church productively?
- What coordination will be necessary to avoid misunderstanding and resentment?
- Who are the people or groups who will be affected, and how can I integrate with them in our common ministry?
- If my call is to a setting outside the local church, how do I then relate to the local church?
- What authority do I have to initiate ministries?
- What authority does my church have in determining the validity/usefulness of my ministry?
- What can I do if the local church does not agree with the ministry my gifts suggest?
- How can I finance and administer ministries if they are not in the budget?

The answers to these questions will differ from place to place. Some gifts and ministries can be applied immediately and without reserve because they are personal qualities and are part of the daily life of the layperson in ministry. Kindness, helpfulness, and encouragement are never out of place and do not require permission from anyone. But not all gifts and the ministries related to them are so uncomplicated. Here are some general precepts:

1. *Gifts identification is between God and the individual Christian, but coordination is important because the use of gifts sometimes affects the life of the church and the community.* Many ministries will fall into place easily, but care should be taken to guard against misunderstanding. A couple in one of the churches I served felt called to minister to youth, but they did not feel comfortable in an institutional setting. They became foster parents and helped a series of young people through critical points in their lives. No permission was required from the church, but they did talk and pray about it with me and with others.

2. *Although the individual Christian has the right to respond to God's call in his or her own way, there must be consideration for the whole body of Christ in every ministry done in its name.* A man from a church I served went to a national meeting of a parachurch ministry group and came back convinced that he had discovered his gifts—they were expressed in the pattern of the ministry he had just learned about. He said that for the first time in his life, he really felt like a Christian. He wanted the entire church to become involved in that model. He was indignant when the board resisted. It is difficult to explain that one person's delight may be another one's boredom. We may have missed a great opportunity, but collective wisdom concluded it was not for us at that time.

3. *If a ministry involves the local church or community, talk with your pastor and the coordinator of small-group ministries.* (If your church does not have a coordinator, suggest that the congregation consider whether one would be right for your church.) Ask for advice and assistance in pursuing opportunities to use your gifts. There may already be ministries in progress that you can join. If not, opportunities may be opened for a new ministry.

Becoming part of a ministry in progress in the local church helps both the people in ministry and the church. In The United Methodist Church, it is no longer necessary for members of teams to be elected by an official body. They may be added to existing teams by the leader or group. The committee on lay leadership (formerly called the committee on nominations and personnel) may help people find teams, and teams find people, at any time.

4. *If you are called to an area of ministry that is not present in your local church, discuss it with your pastor and/or other people or teams who have responsibility for ministries.* Make every effort to avoid conflicts with established ministries or with the primary objectives (mission) of the church. (There are limits to permission giving. For example, anyone reporting a call to set up a chapter of a radical racist group may need some counseling.) While the call supersedes program, much confusion will be avoided if everything is done in consultation with appropriate leaders.

However, those who feel new gifts and calls should resist being appointed to older, inactive groups with a similar name or purpose. Form a new team for new ministries. The sense of call adds passion to ministry, something that many in church organizations have lost. In one church in our area, a member felt the call to establish a ministry for homeless children. The church had no such ministry or team and did not want to make an immediate decision. By the time the council met two months later, the person with the call had already established the ministry, with no relationship to the church.

5. *You may need others to help with the ministry.* Consulting with friends and church leaders and putting notes in church bulletins or newsletters may help find people with similar interests who will join you in ministry. Seek people with a sense of call. Talk with any who respond to explore your vision and theirs.

6. *If you are called to a ministry beyond the local church, in the community or world at large, you may need to add people outside the church to the list of those to be consulted* (community officials, mission boards, existing service organizations, and so forth). Be deliberate. Many promising starts have been thwarted by defiance in the called or resistance by the organized. In the 1970's, a member of the church I was serving felt a strong call to mediate race relations in the community. She spoke to our board, contacted some pastors of other churches of each race, enlisted some people from the university, spoke with the mayor and superintendent of schools, and set up the Community Council on Interracial Harmony. In time much good came of it.

7. *If friends and church officials do not accept your concept for ministry, react with caution.* It may be that you need to give more thought to your response to the call, or perhaps you need time (like Paul) to absorb all the implications of the ministry and get yourself in a right relationship to God and significant people. But, if the call is clear and strong, and if after reflection you feel confident that it is of God, then continue to look for a setting and process for it to become a reality. (Remember Martin Luther and John Wesley? Sometimes separation is necessary.)

8. *Be prepared to work hard.* Do not expect to be funded from budgets. Anyway, most ministries cost little to start if passionate people give their time and resources to it. One young man wanted to start a jail ministry, but his own church was not in favor of it. Then he went to work as a secretary in a local United Methodist church and used his income to help establish the ministry. It is going well and has attracted additional interest and support.

As I have said more than once, this book is about gifts and ministry; but the emphasis is on ministry. It is possible to spend so much time on analysis that nothing gets done. The need is for people to do God's work. But sometimes the urge to do becomes so strong that people forget that not everyone shares their enthusiasm or vision. Those who feel gifted and called are the best candidates to do the work of God, but there are times when passion can become a barrier to successful achievement. Keeping good relationships with people may be a major factor in doing the kind of ministry that our gifts lead us into. (Remember the "one body" in Ephesians 4.)

And remember, above all else, called and gifted people may be a resource for renewal in the local church. It is through them, rather than through church organizations, that we often initiate new ministries. Traditional ministries are so familiar, and we are so used to doing them, that passionate people are necessary to shake things up. Encourage innovation and question traditionalism.

When times and customs change, the church that continues to do the same old things in the same way loses touch with the people it seeks to serve and attract. Church councils tend to propose and support the familiar. And familiarity is said to breed contempt. Voices and ministries from fresh sources are necessary to enliven the church and to bring new people into it.

In churches that maintain a rigid code of procedures and a fixed set of ministry areas, the leadership may become authoritarian instead of enterprising. They defend the status quo and reject the new idea or even the newcomer. Fresh insights, gifts, and ministries can relight the fires.

If we always do the same ministries over and over, it will be difficult to develop new leadership. Leaders and ministries tend to go hand in hand. We do ministry because we have trained leaders to do them, and we have trained leaders because we always do the same ministries. That means that the pool of leadership grows smaller year by year. Fewer people stay involved in ministry. When new gifts and ministries are introduced, the pool of leaders grows and participation increases. Local councils will do well to invite every person to seek God's guidance in founding new ministry opportunities instead of protecting the old organization.

Without the development of new ministry areas, we lose touch with God. Many of the fast-growing independent churches seem more alive and vigorous than our own. One reason may be that they did not have a pattern to follow and went in the direction of what they perceived to be God's call. So they have new worship patterns, new songs, new types of organization, and new miniseries. And they have a new sense of God's immediate presence as the source of it all. They think their motivation is not from Nashville or Anderson or Salt Lake City, but from God.

So they tend to praise the Lord.

Perhaps we can too!

PART 3

A GUIDE FOR EXPLORING AREAS OF MINISTRY

Paragraph 125 in *The Book of Discipline of The United Methodist Church—2000* says that "the heart of Christian ministry is Christ's ministry of outreaching love." This section, titled "The Heart of Christian Ministry," continues: "Christian ministry is the expression of the mind and mission of Christ by a community of Christians that demonstrates a common life of gratitude and devotion, witness and service, celebration and discipleship. *All Christians* are called through their baptism to this ministry of servanthood in the world to the glory of God and for human fulfillment. The forms of this ministry are diverse in locale, in interest, and in denominational accent, yet always catholic [universal] in spirit and outreach."

How do we approach this diverse ministry? How do we, as the body of Christ, make Christ visible in the world? How do we use our gifts and enable others to use their gifts?

Some years ago a group of seventy lay and clergy people in the Holston Conference of The United Methodist Church, with assistance from the General Board of Discipleship, worked over a period of months to develop a description of gifts for ministry and the types of ministry that expressed these gifts. The goal was to provide a groundwork for partnership in ministry between clergy and laity.

We began by considering the task of the church and then looking at specific ministries in which Christ is made visible in the world. While not meant to be exhaustive, the list does provide points of entry for our own use of gifts in ministry in the church and in the world. It is understood that all ministries are open to all people and that both clergy and laity may be called.

The Book of Discipline (¶ 122) describes the process by which disciples fulfill the mission of the church. They

— "proclaim the gospel, seek, welcome and gather persons into the body of Christ;

— lead persons to commit their lives to God through baptism and profession of faith in Jesus Christ;

— nurture persons in Christian living through worship, the sacraments, spiritual disciplines, and other means of grace…;

— send persons into the world to live lovingly and justly as servants of Christ…;

— continue the mission of seeking, welcoming and gathering persons into the community of the body of Christ."

This description suggests that there are four general responsibilities of ministry that might be summarized as to receive, to relate, to equip, and to send. These four elements of ministry form a continuous cycle, a ministry wheel. Each stage is followed by another as long as there is a single person in need of the love of Christ.

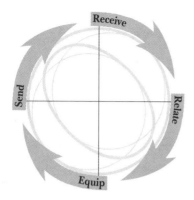

The ministry wheel (illustrated above) is intended to convey two ideas:

- First, there is a connection between the overall purpose of the church and each ministry it supports or promotes. Everything belongs together. Like the gifts, ministries should build up the body of Christ.
- Second, any ministry may relate to any part of the church's purpose. The inner wheel can turn inside the rim so that relational ministries may equip as well as receive; administrative ministries may be those to which we are sent as well as those that equip us to go. Everything is interrelated.

Both clergy and laity are called to ministry. Clergy may live out the call as pastor, educator, missionary, administrator, or community servant. Laity may respond to the call in some of these same ways, but they are also likely to be found in the world—on the farm, in the office, at church or school, or at home. Though their roles may be different, both clergy and laity can claim their gifts and use them.

The ministry descriptions in this section avoid identification with clergy or lay roles. They bypass geographic considerations because each ministry can take place anywhere. We can be in a witness ministry in our own hometown or in Brazil, as a layperson or as an ordained minister, as a commissioned missionary or as an employee in a multinational corporation, in a prestigious high-paying position or in a low-income job. Caring ministries may be realized in the neighborhood where we live or as part of a mission thousands of miles from our community.

We have different names for ministries, depending on where they occur. A person who teaches in church is called a Sunday school teacher; one who teaches in college is called a professor. One who witnesses in local communities may be called an evangelist, but is called a missionary if the witnessing takes place in a foreign country. A provider of care to a transitional community may be a community-service person, but he or she is a consultant or counselor within an affluent community. We sometimes become so interested in the proper terminology that we forget that all ministries are equal, just as all gifts are equal. We carry our ministries in our hearts, whether we are volunteer or paid, lay or professional. We may be called to practice our ministry anywhere.

The ministry descriptions that follow provide simple opportunities that show that anyone can become a minister. None of these forms of ministry requires special permission. They supplement rather than replace the church's organized program, although coordination with church leaders is highly desirable.

The ministries presented in this part of the book explore twelve selected ministry areas. The descriptions in each area include Scriptures to examine as a basis for a particular ministry and a list of activities that could be part of each ministry. You may want to add others as you study.

The ministry areas are deliberately presented in random order to avoid the implication that some are more important than others. You may want to choose one area of ministry for personal investigation. Or you may choose to study all twelve areas in small groups as part of a group retreat, in order to decide which new areas of ministry you or your congregation might want to enter.

Exploring a Ministry

As you read through the twelve ministry area descriptions that follow, remember these general guidelines for developing objectives and strategy as you choose a ministry area to become involved in.

1. Some ministries may be personal and may be practiced anywhere, at any time. They do not need permission or require reports or accountability, except to God. However, it would be wise to discuss your plans with your pastor, coordinator of small groups (see *The Book of Discipline of The United Methodist Church—2000*, ¶ 254), or friends in the church organization. Both individuals and groups may be involved in each area of ministry.
   a. As an individual, you should do the following:
      - Identify an area and a specific ministry that you feel equipped or called to do, such as Spiritual-Growth Ministries: intercessory prayer (Area 5), Wholeness Ministries: serving the lonely and the alienated (Area 9), or Community Ministries: tutoring (Area 11).

- Read the Scriptures suggested for that ministry area.
- Set aside time for prayer, study, and reflection (a requirement for all ministries).
- Consider carefully whether this is actually your area of call. If so, proceed.
- Obtain and/or develop resources that will help you understand and do the ministry.
- Explore opportunities to learn practical skills you may need for the ministry.
- Examine the ministry area for places to begin (for instance, check with school officials to discover where tutors are needed).
- Ask for help if you feel uncertain.
- Encourage feedback from those served and/or from trusted friends or church officials.

b. As a group, you should do the following:
- Discover others with a similar purpose or call and get them together.
- Study the Scriptures and pray with one another.
- Develop a statement of purpose and some general expectations for the group.
- Formulate a covenant among yourselves for doing ministry together. Write it down.
- Develop a strategy for getting started, including expectations of one another.
- Make contact with your pastor, council, or coordinator of small-group ministries.
- Encourage feedback. Review your progress from time to time and adjust as needed.

2. Some ministries may already be part of the church organization, and you can join them.
a. As an individual, you should do the following:
- Examine whether that ministry accurately expresses your own call.
- Determine whether the ministry already exists in some form in the church organization.
- If it does exist, volunteer to become a part of the ministry group. (Remember, election by the church conference is not necessary.) If not, explore the ministry on your own.
- Maintain contact with church leaders to be sure that there is no conflict or overlap, and pursue your ministry with integrity.

b. As a group, you should do the following:
- Clarify the meaning and objectives of the ministry that has been identified.
- Make contact with any groups with similar objectives.

- Determine how both ministries may be pursued, together or separately, without friction.
- Develop a statement of purpose for each group, or for a combined group with a broader focus.
- Make arrangements for a relationship with the church council to ensure both support and an opportunity for review and evaluation.

3. Some ministries may not now be part of the church program and will need careful preparation.
a. If this ministry is entirely new, proceed with caution. Make sure that you and/or the group are perceived to be in legitimate ministry, with Christian motives and objectives in keeping with the mission of the church.
b. Carefully develop a statement of purpose that presents your ministry accurately and enthusiastically.
c. Meet with the pastor or council chair or contact your coordinator of small-group ministries, if you have one, to outline your intentions.
d. Proceed with the ministry, being careful to maintain contacts with others.

4. Some ministries may be beyond the local church and require full coordination with the church and/or any other agencies involved.
a. Examine the community or area to see whether similar ministries exist. If so, consult with them about space and responsibilities to avoid duplication and/or conflict.
b. Obtain and study any information on similar ministries in other areas. Use the information for examples only, not as a substitute for your own ministry vision.
c. Make sure that all legalities are met and that resources are available.
d. Launch your ministry with prayer and confidence.

Each ministry will require its own preparation and processes. Combine the suggestions here with additional suggestions for implementing ministries given in each of the ministry area descriptions to get a full picture of ministry preparation and implementation.

> The ministry descriptions that follow provide simple opportunities for anyone to become a minister. None of them requires special permission. They supplement, rather than replace, the church's organized program, but coordination with church leaders is desirable.

Twelve ministries that are a part of the sections of this ministry cycle are listed on the ministry wheel on this page. This wheel does not include a complete list of possible ministries. You may want to add your favorites to the list as you work through Part 3. However, this list does suggest that there is a place for each person, however gifted, to be a partner with God in ministry to the world.

Ministries That Receive

Worship Ministries: Leading and participating in private and public worship opportunities and in private devotional experiences.

Congregational Care Ministries (Serving): Demonstrating Christian concern and care for people within the congregation and for other people who need comfort, friendship, or personal support.

Relational Ministries (Kindness): Building personal relationships that become channels of God's love and grace wherever we are.

Ministries That Equip

Administrative Ministries (Authority): Ministering through church leadership positions to the people who are part of the organization of the church and the congregation.

Support and Encouragement Ministries (Exhortation): Providing spiritual, social, financial, and/or emotional support for people in mission or in times of stress.

Wholeness Ministries (Healing, Reconciliation): Relating Creator and creation, providing for healing and reconciliation among people, through social structures, and between nations.

Ministries That Relate

Teaching and Learning Ministries (Teaching): Helping people acquire a knowledge of the faith and increasing understanding and skills for ministry.

Spiritual-Growth Ministries (Knowledge, Interpretation): Starting and sustaining experiences for people who are seeking growth in relationship with God.

Helping Ministries: Providing assistance in the functioning of the local church (sacraments, care of buildings, program helps) and to people with special needs.

Ministries That Send

Workplace Ministries (Faith): Relating to people in the workplace in ways that reflect our identity as Christians and our personal and social concern.

Community Ministries (Serving): Being involved in activities that exemplify Christian concern and care for social and personal needs in the surrounding community.

Witness Ministries (Faith, Prophecy): Taking advantage of opportunities and techniques for evangelism and faith sharing in varied settings, at home and around the world.

Gather to Worship; Depart to Serve

Our worship of God is the source of our ministry to the community. Worship is both the environment where many people first encounter God and the experience within which many find support and renewal. It is the universal experience of Christians. Whether in a quiet retreat or in the church's sanctuary, our time spent in deliberate cultivation of the presence of God is essential to both full personhood and discipleship.

This ministry, too, is a shared one. Worship may be planned and led by both clergy and laity. The participation of each in corporate worship is assured through the presence of choirs, ushers, Communion stewards, acolytes, and other conventional servers; but there is also room for lay leadership in reading Scripture, leading in prayer, witnessing, and preaching.

Family devotions, small-group worship, prayer in workplaces and community settings, and personal devotional practices further enlarge the possibilities of a ministry of worship for each of us wherever we are.

Suggestions for Implementing Worship Ministries

1. Become an assistant at worship services: liturgist, usher, greeter, altar guild member, and so forth.

2. If you have musical abilities, offer them to choirs, special worship settings, or classes and groups that meet for worship.

3. Help plan alternative worship services and/or operate computers, sound equipment, projectors, and other aids to worship in special settings.

4. Help your church plan an alternative worship service to serve special groups at times other than the regular Sunday morning service.

5. Help people plan their worship for retreats and other settings. Offer to lead worship yourself if you feel gifted and called to that ministry.

6. Arrange for at-home worship helps for those who cannot attend services. Arrange services in homes for those who would like them, using cassette tapes, broadcasts from the church, or other special opportunities.

Other Opportunities for Worship Ministries

✔ _____

✔ _____

✔ _____

✔ _____

Area I
Worship Ministries

Some Scriptural Sources

Psalm 8; 15; 23; 95; 134

Matthew 6:5-14

John 4:21-24

Romans 12:1-8

1 Corinthians 14:26-33

1 John 4:7-21

Revelation 7:9-17

Types of Activities

✔ Serving as a lay liturgist or leader in church worship

✔ Conducting worship in homes for those who cannot or will not be in church

✔ Leading small groups of peers (church or community) in worship on a regular basis

✔ Planning or participating in community interdenominational worship services

✔ Planning and/or conducting worship in special settings and events

Area 2
Congregational Care Ministries

Some Scriptural Sources

Acts 6:1-7

2 Corinthians 9:10-15

Galatians 6:1-10

Philippians 4:10-20

Colossians 3:12-17

James 2:14-17

Types of Activities

✔ Visiting people who are limited in their ability to leave home

✔ Planning to ensure special attention to people who are in crisis

✔ Providing spiritual and/or physical resources in response to personal needs

✔ Counseling and consulting

✔ Cultivating newcomers or alienated people

✔ Offering sacraments and compassion

✔ Operating a tape ministry (recording the worship services or other activities)

✔ Organizing or working in small groups for support and spiritual growth

Who Cares?

As people are received into the community of faith, they bring both needs that must be cared for and skills in caring. Their needs may be as simple as wishing for a friendly greeting at Sunday worship or as complex as facing a life-threatening illness. Their skills may vary from hand-shaking to crisis counseling. Many members will be involved in demonstrating Christian concern for people in the household of faith—people who are in need of comfort, friendship, or personal support. Others will minister to the whole community, or even the whole world.

Suggestions for Implementing Congregational Care Ministries

1. From personal knowledge, or in consultation with your pastor or other members, identify isolated or unserved groups or people within the congregation.

2. Talk with those people about their needs; then select the needs you can meet.

3. Research what others have done. Read some books on the subject, such as *A Ministry of Caring*, by Duane A. Ewers (Discipleship Resources, 1999); *Can the Pastor Do It Alone?: A Model for Preparing Lay People for Lay Pastoring*, by Melvin J. Steinbron (Gospel Light Publications, 1987); or *Waking to God's Dream: Spiritual Leadership and Church Renewal*, by Dick Wills (Abingdon Press, 1999).

4. Proceed with your personal ministry plans or enlist others to help. This area of need is so great that it is practical to recruit a number of teams for different functions.

Other Opportunities for Congregational Care Ministries

✔ _____

✔ _____

✔ _____

✔ _____

Smile; You Are in Ministry!

O ur day-to-day relationships provide numerous opportunities for ministry. The ties of friendship and kinship create a readiness to express God's love and care. Family, friends, and associates are resources for one another, as are fellow church members. Conversations in many workshops, among both lay and clergy, suggest that the members in our church fellowship are a more important source of support for daily living than are those in other circles. Even the most casual relationships may become a channel for new spiritual life.

Relational ministries are the most personal of all. The intimacy of human interaction makes possible a deeper awareness of the presence of God. We are responsible for seeing that our Christian faith and values are reflected in every level of these interactions.

Suggestions for Implementing Relational Ministries

1. A basic relational ministry is prayer for others. Maintaining a prayer list is one approach. Personal prayers with friends and other personal interactions are also part of this ministry.

2. Remember, not everyone is called to this or any other specific ministry, but even those who are called need to be equipped. Since sensitivity to others is a prerequisite for interpersonal ministry, consider taking a course (many communities offer courses on communications skills) or reading a book such as *Faith Matters: Faith-Mentoring in the Faith Community,* by Sondra Higgins Matthaei (Trinity Press, 1996). (This book is out of print, but it may be found in some libraries.)

3. Learn to listen to those around you, even when they are doing routine things. Reflect on what you hear to provide a base for understanding them.

4. Reflect, alone or in a group, on two or three of your best relationships from the past—with family or with friends. What made the relationships good? What characteristics of those relationships may be used to form other relationships that will allow spiritual energies to flow freely?

5. List ways that you can spiritually support your family, friends, fellow workers, and other members of your congregation. Select ones you feel comfortable doing and practice them mentally so that you will be prepared for the time when they are needed.

6. There is a fine line between helping and interfering, and the line is different from person to person. Sensitivity and skill are required. From each experience learn skills for the next.

7. For training in a wide variety of skills for relational ministries, as well as for congregational care and spiritual-growth ministries, contact Stephen Ministries (see page 77).

Area 3
Relational Ministries

Some Scriptural Sources

Romans 15:1-6; 16:1-16

2 Corinthians 3:1-3

1 John 4:7-21

Types of Activities

✔ Sharing with family members in spiritual inquiry

✔ Being a personal resource to friends in stress and in times of search, sorrow, or celebration

✔ Forming new relationships as a part of outreach

✔ Making covenants with one another for mutual support

Other Opportunities for Relational Ministries

✔ _____

✔ _____

✔ _____

✔ _____

Area 4
Teaching and Learning Ministries

Some Scriptural Sources

Psalm 40:1-8

Micah 4:1-2

Mark 4:13-20

Luke 1:1-4

1 Timothy 4

Types of Activities

✔ Church school classes

✔ Special-purpose learning groups

✔ Self-directed study (books or interactive)

✔ Age-level ministries (children through seniors)

✔ Continuing education in community settings

✔ Bible study groups in church or community

Other Opportunities for Teaching and Learning Ministries

✔ _____

✔ _____

✔ _____

✔ _____

The Learning Organization

The church is committed to joining knowledge and vital piety. One of the greatest dangers to the church's integrity is its members' loss of the urgent need to be informed in both knowledge and practice. A ministry of education brings the learner and the information about the faith together to enrich and enlarge both. Teaching and learning may take place in Sunday school, in small groups, or in regional settings. The future of the church is dependent on its ability to combine history and vision.

Suggestions for Implementing Teaching and Learning Ministries

1. Review the areas and variety of teaching and learning experiences that may be appropriate.

   – Do you have a call to a specific area or topic, such as parenting, spiritual growth, Bible study, world affairs, missions, personal development, youth or children's ministry?

   – Are you interested in finding public learning settings in your field of interest?

2. Evaluate your skills, as an individual or as a group, for learning and teaching functions.

   – Is your basic need for learning together as a group or for networking with others? (Enroll in continuing education in a nearby college.)

   – Do you have the ability to arrange teaching and learning experiences? (Organize classes or groups for special studies.)

   – Are you a good leader in learning situations (lecturing, facilitating discussion, and so forth)? (Recruit and lead special-study or discussion groups.)

3. If you feel called, volunteer to lead existing study groups, Sunday school classes, or special events.

4. If you, as an individual or as a group, feel called to other areas of learning, decide on a method and topic in an atmosphere of spiritual inquiry and prayer.

   – Personal study with sharing among friends (informal discussion group)

   – A short-term or regular group on specific topics chosen by the group

   – A public learning opportunity that you or your group will arrange

   – Helping select curriculum for groups already in place (such as Sunday school classes)

5. Guard against selecting leaders or topics that are inconsistent with the mission or values of your church. Coordinate with the education team or church council.

Our Spiritual Journey

All of us are in a constant process of change. Our relationships to people, organizations, and the natural world are different at various times. Our relationship to God changes as well. A ministry of spiritual growth provides guidance and resources to help people deepen their relationship to God and, through God, to others. Through provision for study, prayer, interaction, and disciplined living, a ministry of spiritual growth can result in richer and more productive discipleship, as well as personal assurance.

Suggestions for Implementing Spiritual-Growth Ministries

1. Pray about your spiritual-growth needs and/or for the spiritual-growth potential of your congregation and community.

2. Develop a prayer discipline of your own and maintain it with care. (*The Upper Room* magazine or other devotional resource may be helpful.)

3. Become familiar with spiritual-growth approaches and settings, especially the small groups based on the Wesley model of class meetings, such as Covenant Discipleship Groups and topical groups based on books or other resources. Consider the United Methodist DISCIPLE Bible study program (Abingdon Press), *The Workbook on Spiritual Disciplines* (Upper Room, 1999), or other books by Maxie Dunnam.

4. Start spiritual-growth activities and/or promote them in the church at large. Small-group activities (based on Wesley's class meetings) and other spiritual-growth activities are strongly supported by most denominational leaders. A recent book by Thomas R. Hawkins, *The Christian Small-Group Leader,* or Grace Bradford's *Guide for Class Leaders* (both from Discipleship Resources) are helpful.

5. If spiritual growth has not been a priority in the past, your calling may be to make it one for the future. Complaining about the lack of spirituality is counterproductive. Helping to encourage it is the task of those called to ministries of spiritual growth.

Other Opportunities for Spiritual-Growth Ministries

✔ _____

✔ _____

✔ _____

✔ _____

Area 5
Spiritual-Growth Ministries

Some Scriptural Sources

Job 42:1-6

Psalm 8; 23; 27; 46; 63; 105; 109

Proverbs 4:1-8

1 Corinthians 13:11-13

Ephesians 4:17-32

Types of Activities

✔ Disciplined Bible study

✔ Participating in and leading spiritual-growth groups

✔ Spiritual life retreats and inter-relational worship

✔ Intercessory prayer chains

✔ Personal or shared devotional exercises

✔ Covenant groups for study and/or prayer

✔ Theological study and reflection

Area 6
Helping Ministries

Some Scriptural Sources

Matthew 5:38-42

Mark 9:33-37

Acts 6:1-7

2 Thessalonians 3:6-12

1 Timothy 3:8-13

Types of Activities

✔ Telephone contacts to promote events

✔ Bulletin boards or other displays

✔ Extra office help for newsletters, phones, Easter/Christmas letters, and so forth

✔ Childcare for meetings

✔ Setting up rooms, providing refreshments and other services for meetings

✔ Transportation for people with physical disabilities, the elderly, and so forth

Where There's a Will...

From its beginnings, the church has been a community of people formed by the work of God, animated by the Holy Spirit, and sustained by the worship and service of its members. Christian community is based on the willingness of all members to accept responsibility, individually and corporately, to respond to the needs and rights of others. This is known as helping ministries.

Helping can be anything from serving as ushers or greeters, to preparing the sanctuary for the worship services, to answering phones and stuffing envelopes, to providing resources to people with disabilities. Helping ministries can best be discovered by asking the question, "What needs to be done in the church and community, and which of these things can I do best?"

Suggestions for Implementing Helping Ministries

1. Do not disdain this call. Some may fail to understand how vital a ministry of helping can be. The variety of opportunities is unlimited. For those who do not need or seek the limelight, helping ministries can become a satisfying experience of gift sharing.

2. Many helping activities can occur spontaneously without being noticed, such as tidying the sanctuary. Even so, helping ministries are necessary to provide support and foundations for more-visible ministries.

3. Look for opportunities for structured help (providing transportation for people with special needs, mowing the church lawn, or working in a telephone ministry).

4. Helping services require no permission, but they often need coordination with others.

Other Opportunities for Helping Ministries

✔ _____

✔ _____

✔ _____

✔ _____

Let My People Go!

A basic task of leaders is to set people free to serve God (Exodus 8:1). Those who are gifted in administration are often able to discern abilities and gifts in others. They are good at enabling people to minister by creating the conditions in which skills and talents may be used effectively. We sometimes try to separate administration and ministry, but they are parts of one whole. Administrators are ministers helping ministers to minister.

The best administrators are concerned for the spiritual empowerment of each person in the organization. By helping individuals realize their highest spiritual potential, administrators not only serve the needs of the congregation and its ministry but also become catalysts for the work of the Holy Spirit in personal growth and development.

Suggestions for Implementing Administrative Ministries

1. Meet with others to talk about what it means to say that serving on church boards, committees, and teams is really a spiritual endeavor.

2. Be insightful enough to accept those positions to which you feel called. Of course, administration may be a call in itself, and some people may feel comfortable in many different administrative roles.

3. Transform every organizational task into a spiritual assignment. Transcend political considerations and petty jockeying for power or influence.

4. Pray with and for those who share official duties with you. Always remember for whom you work, and that Christ is the real administrator.

5. Support other officials, and give way for new ones as they emerge.

Other Opportunities for Administrative Ministries

✔ _____

✔ _____

✔ _____

✔ _____

Area 7
Administrative Ministries

Some Scriptural Sources

Numbers 11:16-17

John 15

Acts 15:6-21; 18:24-28

1 Corinthians 3:5-23; 12:12-31

Philippians 1:27-30

1 Timothy 3:1-7

Types of Activities

✔ Serving on councils, committees, and teams

✔ Identifying people with gifts and helping equip them for ministry

✔ Providing leadership for programs, ministries, and planning events

✔ Overseeing areas of church maintenance and facilities improvement

Area 8
Support and Encouragement Ministries

Some Scriptural Sources

Matthew 25:31-40

Romans 12:14-21; 15:1-6

Galatians 6:1-5

Types of Activities

✔ Making phone calls (care-ring) to people recuperating from surgery or illness

✔ Providing support to those with serious, long-term, or terminal illness

✔ Recruiting people to provide and promote support for a missionary

✔ Forming a group to talk and pray with community leaders in times of change or stress

✔ Organizing prayer and sharing groups for families in crisis

✔ Establishing marriage encounter/enrichment groups, Alcoholics Anonymous, Al-Anon, support groups, and so forth

Thanks for the Ministry!

Encouragement and support are basic to the continuity of our ministry throughout the church. These ministries undergird activities in the congregation, in the community, and around the world. We encourage one another in many ways, from individual encounters to specialized support groups for people in community leadership or distant fields of mission.

Offering support is a natural expression of ministry by people who have the gifts of kindness, encouragement, understanding, or healing. Perhaps more than any of the others, this ministry is a function of personal characteristics. Some people naturally are more sensitive, have more tact, and are more positive in their reactions to others. They can encourage without appearing critical, can sympathize without appearing patronizing, can discuss experiences without condescending. While conscious development of these characteristics is possible, it is rare.

For those who have these skills, a world of opportunity awaits, although often without recognition or gratitude. Family, friends, fellow workers, church members, new Christians, and chance acquaintances can be strengthened and renewed by the judicious use of support and encouragement skills in times of new experiences, self-doubt, or stress. Leaders may need such encouragement and support most of all, both as a reassurance in times of achievement and as a resource when things are going badly. Many have reported that at some time they have been prevented from succumbing to egotism or rescued from despair by an encouraging word.

Suggestions for Implementing Support and Encouragement Ministries

1. Be aware of people who have spiritual, personal life, or business critical needs. Pray for them, listen and respond, express reassurance and confidence.

2. Select a missionary to support not only financially but also with prayer and encouragement.

3. Show appreciation to a city official or to public servants (mayor, social worker, school teacher).

4. Write letters and send cards to those who are away at school or who are unable to attend worship because of illness or a disability.

5. Work with someone who is good at administrative skills to form a support group for people who are facing life crises.

Other Opportunities for Support and Encouragement Ministries

✔ _____

✔ _____

✔ _____

CREATOR, CREATION, CREATURES

Christ promised wholeness: the healing of bodies and minds, the reconciliation of fragmented humankind, the harmony of the universe. The coming of Christ was the promise made visible. The world, created by God, was to be reunited with its Creator in response to the redemptive act on the cross. Lives have been saved. People are less barbaric. The earth is more hospitable. Healing and reconciliation are everywhere in process, yet are needed everywhere. This ministry demands the best of each of us; and for the especially gifted, it may demand all.

The ministry of wholeness is in response to the call to heal failing bodies, tormented minds, fragmented societies, threatened creatures, ravaged land. Its aim is to assist in the reconciliation of all creation to the one who made it, God.

Suggestions for Implementing Wholeness Ministries

1. Be sensitive to the risks of answering the call to wholeness ministries: (a) possible divisions over social and religious objectives; (b) social alienation, which may result from advocacy and social reform; and (c) a focus on economic gain, leading people to greed and self-interest.

2. For the person or the group, one of the first activities should be a prayerful, thoughtful consideration of what differentiates ministry from exploitation.

3. Define specific ministries that will best express the need to restore wholeness. First decide whether to plan for a vocation or a volunteer ministry. Then separate the spiritual from the political-social elements.

4. The call may be for a lifetime, but choosing a focus may occur more than once. Your focus may be health careers (nurses, physicians, hospital workers), advocacy (working for racial equality, fair treatment for workers, protection of the environment), nurture (taking care of the victims of social and pathological disorders), reconciliation (bringing unity, rescuing the alienated, working for peace). Or some may focus on a prayer and support role rather than on an active one.

5. Since most of these areas demand training and experience, there may be time between choice and ministry. But for the truly called, the wait will be worthwhile.

6. As with any area of ministry, you must choose whether your calling is to focus on a prayer and support role or on an active role in wholeness ministries. Each person called to wholeness ministries must choose the level of involvement according to life circumstances.

Other Opportunities for Wholeness Ministries

✔ _____

✔ _____

AREA 9
WHOLENESS MINISTRIES

SOME SCRIPTURAL SOURCES

Genesis 1; 2

Psalm 8; 24; 104; 121

Acts 17:22-31

Romans 8:12-39

2 Corinthians 5:16-21

Colossians 1:15-20

TYPES OF ACTIVITIES

✔ Praying for the healing of people, relationships, nations

✔ Working for peace and reconciliation

✔ Working for racial and cultural inclusiveness

✔ Advocating justice for all people

✔ Practicing physical or mental-health disciplines

✔ Providing hunger and nutrition services

✔ Conserving natural resources

✔ Providing support and restoration for victims of personal and social abuse

✔ Encouraging humane treatment of animals

✔ Fighting against substance abuse

✔ Ministering to the lonely and alienated

Area 10
Workplace Ministries

Some Scriptural Sources

Exodus 23:1-9

Psalm 41:1-3

Matthew 6:1-4

Luke 10:25-37

Romans 12:9-16

1 John 3:11-18

Types of Activities

✔ Befriending fellow workers

✔ Helping to develop a supportive atmosphere

✔ Protecting workers from exploitation

✔ Forming or attending prayer and/or study sessions at work

✔ Offering fellow workers Christ when it is appropriate

Christ in the Midst

For most adults, much of our daily life is spent in a work environment. Whether it is in the home, in industry or business settings, or traveling from city to city, most of us have a workplace. There we experience success, failure, relaxation, stress, and personal growth and decline—all of which affect our whole life. Our direction in life itself sometimes seems dependent on our feelings about our work.

The workplace is one arena where we live out the gospel. We affirm or deny the gospel by what we are, how we relate to others, and what values we represent. Along with our family, social, and church experiences, our witness in the workplace can reveal the meaning and depth of our Christian commitment.

Ministry in the workplace may be more a product of who we are than of what we do. Our identity among our fellow workers—our reliability, compassion, and openness to others—may be the only ministry we have or need to have. But there may be other opportunities as well that can help us enlarge our ministry.

Suggestions for Implementing Workplace Ministries

1. In a church class, community group, or group recruited to talk about faith and your occupation, discuss some of the Scriptures listed on this page. Talk about the experiences of places where group members work. Answer the question, "What does it mean to be Christian where I work?" Some may even want to write their answer in a paragraph.

2. Alone or in a group, compile a set of principles that form a philosophy of Christian presence in the workplace, within the congregation, or in the community. Invite people to respond. Consider these four possible workplace ministry channels, each of which can be a witness of our Christian experience and commitment:
   a. ministry of helpfulness—the person who does things for others, helps the hurting, assists processes;
   b. ministry of communication—listening, responding, opening communications, saying the right things, helping work things through;
   c. ministry of ethics—examining, reflecting on, and modeling moral values and ethical behavior;
   d. ministry of change—providing rationale and processes for improving relationships and productivity, helping people change, and helping people accept change.

3. Answer the workplace questionnaire, on page 71, for yourself. Talk with fellow workers about filling it out for themselves and for one another.
   • How do you rate yourself?
   • How do others rate you?
   • Reflect on what this means for your Christian presence in the workplace.

Take the results of these examinations to work with you. Make your Christian presence felt in a nonthreatening way.

In My Workplace	Seldom	Sometimes	Usually
1. I am considered compatible.	____	____	____
2. I am dependable.	____	____	____
3. I respond to friendly overtures.	____	____	____
4. I am helpful to others.	____	____	____
5. I am identified as a Christian.	____	____	____
6. I treat others fairly.	____	____	____
7. I am a good listener.	____	____	____
8. I have high ethical standards.	____	____	____
9. I carry my share of the work.	____	____	____

Other Opportunities for Workplace Ministries

✔ _____

✔ _____

✔ _____

✔ _____

Area II
Community
Ministries

Some Scriptural Sources

Amos 5:21-24

Matthew 6:1-4; 25:31-46

Luke 4:16-21; 10:25-37

1 John 3:11-18

Types of Activities

✔ Public school tutoring

✔ Emergency assistance to those in need

✔ Meals on Wheels, clothes closets, food banks

✔ Counseling services

✔ Community improvement organizations, community politics

✔ Daycare and childcare facilities

✔ Volunteer work with community agencies

✔ Service with and for the unemployed

✔ Contact telephone ministries

✔ Refugee services

✔ Migrant ministries

On the Street Where You Live

Wherever we are, a community surrounds us—whether in a village in Mexico, in a suburb in Kansas, or in a small town in Virginia. These geographical communities are both complicated and enriched by other communities: the vocational community, the religious community, the social community, the political community. Each community has a multitude of opportunities and needs that differ, depending on the age and socio-economic level of the people, the stability of the community, the geographic circumstances, and the social and religious factors. Some Christians are especially gifted to serve the needs of people in the communities where they are. As we provide physical, economic, and emotional resources, we participate in the ministry of servanthood.

It is a mistake to assume that needy communities are only those with visible economic deficiencies. Pain, stress, and loneliness can be as present in an affluent suburb as in a poverty-stricken village. As we provide physical, economic, and emotional resources, we can reflect the ministry of servanthood wherever we are.

Suggestions for Implementing Community Ministries

1. You may be attracted to a community ministry that already exists and choose to participate in that ministry. Or you may explore a ministry for a group not presently served by anyone else in your community.

2. Whether alone or in a group, learn the needs of the group you choose to serve. Plan for personal contact with members of the group. Read about the group and talk with others experienced in working with that group.

3. After consulting with appropriate people in the church and in the community, explore the ministry:
   a. Give attention to the personnel needed and where they are available.
   b. Look for a suitable site and buildings, if needed.
   c. Consider the need for funding carefully. Of course, not every ministry needs large sums, and some may require none. But raising money is not difficult if the ministry is appealing.
   d. Pray throughout for guidance and fortitude.

Other Opportunities for Community Ministries

✔ _____

✔ _____

✔ _____

✔ _____

Go Tell It On the Mountain!

Area 12
Witness Ministries

Telling the good news is the first ministry of the church, whether it is in the form of evangelistic outreach or reassurance for those already in the fold. Both individuals and the body of believers are called to witness to the Christian faith and Christian experience.

Both clergy and laity think that witness is a shared responsibility. Neither group is more important than the other. Each has an indispensable place in the ministry of witness. We are all called to tell the good news. (For United Methodists, there is no greater proof than Harry Denman, a layperson, as the leader of the General Board of Evangelism for many years.)

Suggestions for Implementing Witness Ministries

1. Witnessing is sometimes presented as the only task of the church. However, Scripture clearly calls Christians to many facets of servanthood. Witness (evangelism) is important, but it is not always easy to separate witness from other activities. All of the other eleven ministries described in these pages may at times serve as evangelistic opportunities. And there are so many forms of witness that we may have difficulty deciding which of them is best for us. We may need some guidance.

2. Encourage a small group in your church to use the resource *Witness: Exploring and Sharing Your Christian Faith,* by Dr. Ronald K. Crandall (Discipleship Resources, 2001). This twenty-five week study of the Christian faith can increase your confidence as you talk with others about your faith.

3. Others may want to read the book *Faith-Sharing: Dynamic Christian Witnessing by Invitation (Revised and Expanded),* by H. Eddie Fox and George E. Morris (Discipleship Resources, 1996). This classic introduction to Christian witness has served many people well.

4. Personal evangelism can be implemented anywhere. Talk about your faith with friends and strangers in any place. No special language or skills are necessary. In fact, the most effective witness is the sincere one, rather than the one with a practiced approach and polished speech.

5. You may prefer to be part of a local church witness group sent out by the church to cultivate new members and win others for Christ. In fact, if your church does not have such a group, you might start one.

6. It is also possible to initiate group evangelism through a revival or through a Lay Witness Mission experience. *A Journey of Faith: Lay Witness Mission Handbook* (Discipleship Resources, 2001), a handbook for a Lay Witness Mission event, is available from the General Board of Discipleship of The United Methodist Church.

Other Opportunities for Witness Ministries

✔ _____

✔ _____

Some Scriptural Sources

Psalm 66:1-9

Isaiah 6:1-8

Matthew 28:16-20

Mark 6:6-12

Acts 11:19-21

Romans 15:1-6

Philippians 1:12-26

2 Timothy 1:8-10; 4:1-5

Types of Activities

✔ Personal witness in appropriate situations

✔ Ministries in prisons and institutions

✔ Home visitation by trained teams to offer Christ

✔ Media presentations that promote or support Christ and Christianity

✔ Organized evangelism where needed

Other Ministries

Doing ministry based on the gifts is the natural purpose of each Christian life. However, nothing is automatic about the identification of gifts, the choice of ministries, or the approach to service. All of these are to be discovered, developed, and deployed as befits the work of God in the world. Each place and each era will find its own gifts to fit its own needs—all within the framework of the plan of God. We are seekers, looking for the place we fit and the means by which we become ministers, through the grace of God. In that sense we are all charismatics—full of grace—and all servants of the most high.

What other ministries might you add to these twelve ministries areas based on your own gifts or the gifts of others in your congregation?

Ministry Area

Gifts

Scripture References

Types of Activities

Ministry Area

Gifts

Scripture References

Types of Activities

Ministry Area

Gifts

Scripture References

Types of Activities

Ministry Area

Gifts

Scripture References

Types of Activities

Ministry Area

Gifts

Scripture References

Types of Activities

Ministry Area

Gifts

Scripture References

Types of Activities

PART 4

RECOMMENDED RESOURCES FOR YOUR EXPLORATION

GENERAL RESOURCES

- *Accountable Discipleship: Living in God's Household,* by Steven W. Manskar (Nashville: Discipleship Resources, 2000).
- *Body Building: Creating a Ministry Team Through Spiritual Gifts* ("Leadership Insight Series"), by Brian Kelley Bauknight (Nashville: Abingdon Press, 1996).
- *Dancing With Dinosaurs: Ministry in a Hostile and Hurting World,* by William Easum (Nashville: Abingdon Press, 1993).
- *Equipped for Every Good Work: Building a Gifts-Based Church,* by Dan R. Dick and Barbara Miller (Nashville: Discipleship Resources, 2001).
- *The Equipping Pastor: A Systems Approach to Congregational Leadership,* by R. Paul Stevens (Bethesda, MD: The Alban Institute, 1993).
- *Gifts of the Spirit,* by Kenneth Cain Kinghorn (Nashville: Abingdon Press, 1976).
- *Lay Speaking Ministries* Basic Course and Advanced Courses, various topics (Nashville: Discipleship Resources).
- *Making the Church Work: Converting the Church for the 21st Century* (Second Edition), by Edward H. Hammett (Macon: Smith and Helwys, 2000).
- *Network: Understanding God's Design for You in the Church,* by Bruce Bugbee, Don Cousins, and Bill Hybels (Grand Rapids: Zondervan, 1994).
- *Partners in Ministry: Clergy and Laity,* by Roy W. and Jackie B. Trueblood (Nashville: Abingdon Press, 1999).
- *Rediscovering Our Spiritual Gifts,* by Charles V. Bryant (Nashville: Upper Room, 1991).
- *Seeking and Doing God's Will: Discernment for the Community of Faith,* by Garrie Stevens, Pamela Lardear, and Sharon Duger (Nashville: Discipleship Resources, 1998).
- *Selecting Church Leaders: A Practice in Spiritual Discernment,* by Charles M. Olsen and Ellen Morseth (Nashville: Upper Room, 2002).
- *The Stones That the Builders Rejected: The Development of Ethical Leadership From the Black Church Tradition,* edited by Walter Earl Fluker (Harrisburg, PA: Trinity Press International, 1998).
- *The Web of Women's Leadership: Recasting Congregational Ministry,* by Susan Willhauck and Jacqulyn Thorpe (Nashville: Abingdon Press, 2001).
- "Vital Ministry in the Small-Membership Church" series (Nashville: Discipleship Resources).

Worship Ministries

- *A Community of Joy: How to Create Contemporary Worship* ("Effective Church Series"), by Timothy Wright (Nashville: Abingdon Press, 1994).

- *Contemporary Worship for the 21st Century: Worship or Evangelism?* by Daniel T. Benedict and Craig Kennet Miller (Nashville: Discipleship Resources, 1994).

- *Worship & Daily Life: A Resource for Worship Planners*, edited by Aileen Williams (Nashville: Discipleship Resources, 1999).

- *Worship Matters: A United Methodist Guide to Ways to Worship (Volume I)* and *Worship Matters: A United Methodist Guide to Worship Work (Volume II)*, edited by E. Byron Anderson (Nashville: Discipleship Resources, 1999).

Congregational Care Ministries

- *Can the Pastor Do It Alone?: A Model for Preparing Lay People for Lay Pastoring*, by Melvin J. Steinbron (Ventura, CA: Gospel Light Publications, 1987).

- *A Ministry of Caring*, by Duane A. Ewers (Nashville: Discipleship Resources, 1999).

- *Waking to God's Dream: Spiritual Leadership and Church Renewal*, by Dick Wills (Abingdon Press, 1999).

Relational Ministries

- *The Christian Small-Group Leader*, by Thomas R. Hawkins (Nashville: Discipleship Resources, 2001).

- *Guide for Class Leaders: A Model for Christian Formation*, by Grace Bradford (Nashville: Discipleship Resources, 1999).

- *Relational Refugees: Alienation and Reincorporation in African American Churches and Communities*, by Edward P. Wimberly (Nashville: Abingdon Press, 2000).

Teaching and Learning Ministries

- *Foundations: Shaping the Ministry of Christian Education in Your Congregation* (Nashville: Discipleship Resources, 1993).

- *Keeping in Touch: Christian Formation and Teaching*, by Carol F. Krau (Nashville: Discipleship Resources, 1999).

- "What Every Teacher Needs to Know" series (Nashville: Discipleship Resources, 2002).

Spiritual-Growth Ministries

- *The Christian Small-Group Leader*, by Thomas R. Hawkins (Nashville: Discipleship Resources, 2001).

- *Connecting With God: 14 Ways Churches Can Help People Grow Spiritually*, by Herb Miller (Nashville: Abingdon Press, 1994).

- *Guide for Class Leaders: A Model for Christian Formation*, by Grace Bradford (Nashville: Discipleship Resources, 1999).

- *The Heart's Journey: Christian Spiritual Formation in the Life of a Small Group*, by Barb Nardi Kurtz (Nashville: Discipleship Resources, 2001).

Helping Ministries

- *Safe Sanctuaries: Reducing the Risk of Child Abuse in the Church*, by Joy Thornburg Melton (Nashville: Discipleship Resources, 1998).

Administrative Ministries

- *The Buck Stops Here: Legal and Ethical Responsibilities for United Methodist Organizations*, by Mary Logan (Nashville: Discipleship Resources, 2000).

- *Faithful Leadership: Learning to Lead With Power*, by Thomas R. Hawkins (Nashville: Discipleship Resources, 1999).

Support and Encouragement Ministries

- *The Heart's Journey: Christian Spiritual Formation in the Life of a Small Group*, by Barb Nardi Kurtz (Nashville: Discipleship Resources, 2001).

- *A Ministry of Caring*, by Duane A. Ewers (Nashville: Discipleship Resources, 1999).

- *Waking to God's Dream: Spiritual Leadership and Church Renewal*, by Dick Wills (Nashville: Abingdon Press, 1999).

Wholeness Ministries

- *Blessed to Be a Blessing: How to Have an Intentional Healing Ministry in Your Church*, by James K. Wagner (Nashville: Upper Room, 1991).

- *Cultivating Christian Community,* by Thomas R. Hawkins (Nashville: Discipleship Resources, 2001).

- *World Peas: And Other Ways to Make a Difference,* edited by Rebekah Chevalier (Etobicoke, Ontario: United Church of Canada, 1999).

Workplace Ministries

- *Equipping the Saints: Mobilizing Laity for Ministry,* edited by Michael J. Christenson with Carl E. Savage (Nashville: Abingdon Press, 2000).

- *The Ministry of the Laity,* by James D. Anderson and Ezra Earl Jones (New York: HarperCollins, 1986).

Community Ministries

- *NextChurch.Now: Creating New Faith Communities,* by Craig Kennet Miller (Nashville: Discipleship Resources, 2000).

- *Pentecost Journey: A Planning Guide for Hispanic Ministries,* by Jeannie Treviño-Teddlie (Nashville: Discipleship Resources, 1999).

Witness Ministries

- *Faith-Sharing: Dynamic Christian Witnessing by Invitation (Revised & Expanded),* by H. Eddie Fox and George E. Morris (Nashville: Discipleship Resources, 1996).

- *A Journey of Faith: Lay Witness Mission Handbook* (Nashville: Discipleship Resources, 2001).

- *Witness: Exploring and Sharing Your Christian Faith,* by Ronald K. Crandall (Nashville: Discipleship Resources, 2001).

Other Resources

- **The General Board of Discipleship of The United Methodist Church**
  P.O. Box 340003
  Nashville, TN 37203-0003
  Phone (toll free): 877-899-2780
  Web: www.gbod.org
  (Resources and consultation on all subjects in this book)

- **Stephen Ministries**
  2045 Innerbelt Business Center Dr.
  St. Louis, MO 63114-5765
  Phone: 314-428-2600
  Web: www.stephenministries.org
  (The Stephen Series, with training for ministries to individuals and groups with special needs; The ChristCare Series, training for a small-group ministry system)

- **The Alban Institute**
  Suite 1250 West
  7315 Wisconsin Avenue
  Bethesda, MD 20814
  Phone (toll free): 800-486-1318
  E-mail: education@alban.org
  Web: www.alban.org
  (Books, materials, seminars, and consulting for congregations, especially lay-clergy relationships)